More Praise for *The Tasti D-Lite Way*

"With social media invading the sanctity of traditional marketing in retail brands today, how can we judge its impact? Well here is how. . . . In their new book, Jim Amos and BJ Emerson provide real-life insights and results relating to this new phenomenon. Jim is one of world's best leaders at building brands and being at the forefront of trends . . . and *The Tasti D-Lite Way* is an example of how to turn the advent of social media into understandable, actionable strategies. Digest its rich content and you will find loyal customers lining up!"

> —*Jon Luther, Chairman, Dunkin' Brands (Dunkin' Donuts, Baskin Robbins) and Chairman, Arby's Inc.*

"*The Tasti D-Lite Way* is not a book about franchising. Nor is it another social media book. It's a book about brand fanaticism that began with *Sex and the City* and grew through unsolicited television appearances, customer-driven Facebook groups, tweets, evangelists, and blogs, resulting in not just national but international expansion of a New York–centric phenomenon. Amos and Emerson tell the Tasti D-Lite story in a D-Liteful way that will teach you about business growth, expansion, brand evangelists, and listening—really listening—to what your customers, competition, and detractors have to say about you on the web. If you lead a business or are considering entrepreneurship, buy and read this book now."

> —*Gini Dietrich, CEO, Arment Dietrich and coauthor of* Marketing in the Round

"If there was ever a restaurant company prepared to exploit social media, it is Tasti D-Lite. Having developed an almost cult-like following through delivery of a great tasting product, Tasti D-Lite identified the power of social media to maximize its brand and cement its customer loyalty. This book tells the story of how marketing and technology worked hand-in-hand to help position the company for growth. Tasti D-Lite leveraged its success through the convergence of customer loyalty programs, social media, and the emergence of mobile technology."

> —*David Matthews, SVP and CIO, National Restaurant Association*

"As a business, you can always get advice from a consultant, listen to a guru, or read a blog. However, getting valuable, actionable advice based on the experience of a brand that has been there and done it, now that is priceless. The team at Tasti D-Lite aren't telling you what they THINK might work, they are sharing what they KNOW works. I highly recommend this book for any brand or business looking to understand the work it takes to build loyalty in the world of the Social Consumer."

—*Simon Salt, CEO, IncSlingers and*
author of Social Location Marketing

"For any brand interested in understanding the convergence of digital, social media, and customer loyalty, *The Tasti D-Lite Way* is the 'how to' book you've been looking for. I am consistently amazed at the job the folks at Tasti-D have done in successfully combining the art of innovation and customer know-how to create the winning formula of engaging and 'd-lite-ing' customers."

—*Aaron Strout, Head of Location-Based Marketing, WCG and*
coauthor of Location-Based Marketing for Dummies

"Two of my favorite things in life are Tasti D-Lite and social media. Now I can consume both in book form. *The Tasti-D-Lite Way* shows how an industry can be disrupted when a socially savvy marketer partners with a forward-thinking CEO to integrate technology with purpose into a business. Read this book with a swirl of Cake Batter and Oreos 'n Cream to sweeten the learnings."

—*Rachel Tipograph, Director, Global Digital and*
Social Media, Gap Inc.

"Jim and BJ offer a rare gift, sharing timeless wisdom and very practical advice based on their groundbreaking experiences at Planet Tasti. As our physical and virtual worlds merge and the value pendulum swings back to local, authentic engagements, Jim and BJ remind us that people, character, and culture are all that matter and teach how technology can be a great enabler to treat individuals—whether consumers, franchisees, associates, or stakeholders—how they want to be treated. Don't miss it!"

—*Nathan Estruth, Vice President, Procter & Gamble FutureWorks*

"*The Tasti D-Lite Way* is much more than the story of how social media helped Tasti D-Lite become incredibly successful. It's a how-to book that connects the three most essential ingredients to success in today's connected world—the customer experience, the platform to share it, and the longing for belonging (community). Jim Amos and BJ Emerson get it right by making the customer experience the nonnegotiable foundation that everything else is built on. Finally, a book that combines the timeless truths of a successful business with the most practical and strategic tools that social media provides."

—Tom Ziglar, CEO, Ziglar Inc.

"Jim and BJ have outlined what every growing business craves— creative ways to reach consumers and form an emotional connection at a reasonable cost."

—Bill Fry, Chairman, Oreck and Operating Partner, American Securities Private Equity Group

"The Tasti D-Lite story is edible proof that brands can deliver authentic relationships without sacrificing revenue. Whether it's interactive technology or innovative leadership, the collective wisdom of BJ and Jim provides an easy-to-follow blueprint for a hard-to-swallow concept: listening to customers actually works! Read it, live it, and pass it on."

—Adrian Parker, Social, Mobile, and Emerging Media, Intuit

"*The Tasti-D-Lite Way* is an invaluable resource for marketers and operators alike. Nowhere else have I seen such concrete understanding of basic franchise business principles and thorough working knowledge of mobile, social, and location-based thinking displayed in a concise and thought-provoking manner. The book is a unique guide into the true inner workings of a business and its efforts to use the latest in technology and tactics to stand out from the crowd. And it's not just theory; they've done it, proved it, and proved it yet again! There are case studies and then there is the book—this is it."

—Asif R. Khan, Founder and President, Location-Based Marketing Association

"Learn from one of the true early adopters of transparency on the web. The Tasti D-Lite product is nothing short of phenomenal in the real world and the same is true of its social media marketing in the virtual world. This book demonstrates the detail behind that transparency which has led to its success in ways few other brands are willing to share publicly. If you're developing your personal or business brand, this 'how-we-did-it' book is a must-read."

—*Todd Leiser, Director of Franchise Sales,*
Valpak Direct Marketing Systems, Inc.

"Need help opening the 'cyber door'—transitioning from traditional media to social media? Well, Jim and BJ bust the door wide open. Their story of Tasti D-Lite, one of America's most beloved franchises, is laced with practical, easy-to-execute strategies. This must-read book is every franchisee's road map to social media success."

—*Wayne Breitbarth, author of* The Power Formula for LinkedIn
Success: Kick-Start Your Business, Brand, and Job Search

"New media professionals have long recognized Tasti D-Lite's innovative and highly effective use of social media, and they will no doubt want to devour every word of *The Tasti D-Lite Way: Social Media Marketing Lessons for Building Loyalty and a Brand Customers Crave*. Written by the architects of the company's online strategy, Jim Amos and BJ Emerson, this book explains how businesses can work with the inherent biases of the new media, going with the flow that favors transparency, active participation on the part of audiences and consumers, and the building of powerful, long-lasting relationships with customers. The contemporary media environment represents a radical reversal of many of the ways that business previously was conducted, and the choice we face today is either to be swept away by the social media tsunami or to learn how to surf the digital tidal wave. Amos and Emerson provide an intelligible, down-to-earth, and altogether enlightening account of how businesses can survive and thrive through a thorough understanding of our new world of online communications and social networks."

—*Lance Strate, Professor of Communication and*
Media Studies and Director of the Professional Studies
in New Media Program, Fordham University

Social Media Marketing Lessons *for*
Building Loyalty and a Brand Customers Crave

The

tasti D·lite®
Way

James Amos, Jr.
BJ Emerson

New York Chicago San Francisco Lisbon London Madrid Mexico City
Milan New Delhi San Juan Seoul Singapore Sydney Toronto

1 2 3 4 5 6 7 8 9 0   QFR/QFR   1 8 7 6 5 4 3 2

ISBN   978-0-07-179937-9
MHID   0-07-179937-0

e-ISBN 978-0-07-179938-6
e-MHID   0-07-179938-9

Library of Congress Cataloging-in-Publication Data

Amos, James.
    The Tasti D-Lite way : social media marketing lessons for building loyalty and a brand customers crave / by James Amos and BJ Emerson.
      p. cm.
    ISBN-13: 978-0-07-179937-9 (alk. paper)
    ISBN-10: 0-07-179937-0 (alk. paper)
    1. Internet marketing. 2. Social media. 3. Branding (Marketing) 4. Customer loyalty. 5. Tasti D-Lite (Firm) I. Emerson, BJ II. Title.
    HF5415.1265.A46 2013
    658.8'72—dc23
                                                                    2012025366

Interior design by THINK Book Works.

McGraw-Hill books are available at special quantity discounts to use as premiums and sales promotions or for use in corporate training programs. To contact a representative, please e-mail us at bulksales@mcgraw-hill.com.

This book is printed on acid-free paper.

CONTENTS

ACKNOWLEDGMENTS

The journey of a brand involves many. *The Tasti D-Lite Way* is a collective mindset and effort of numerous participants who share the vision of what the brand can become. While we greatly appreciate all those we were able to include within this text, there are many others who are part of the Tasti D-Lite story whom we also wish to thank.

To the many passionate Tasti D-Lite fans who have carried this amazing brand over the years and for those now patiently waiting in new markets for its arrival, we thank you.

To Snow Phipps for standing behind Tasti D-Lite and having the vision to take it into the future.

Thanks to all our vendor partners, associates, domestic franchisees, area developers and master franchisees around the world who are helping to make Tasti D-Lite a global brand.

Special thanks go out to those friends and industry partners who contributed their depth of insight and expertise for this book.

We'd also like to recognize all the supportive and encouraging folks at McGraw-Hill who didn't want to publish just another book on social media.

We are grateful to our literary agent Jessica Faust for seeing this through with us and believing in what could be.

To those authors, bloggers, and journalists who have included us in their works and have inspired us to write this story, we thank you.

Special thanks to our families who also share the vision and support us in this journey.

PROLOGUE

When it comes to customer loyalty, there is no final destination. It is a journey. Loyalty is relational and emotional, and, like all relationships, it must be worked on to be maintained. Capturing and holding onto the heart of today's empowered consumer is a journey requiring constant change and an intentional pursuit of relevance in the marketplace.

In many regards, this is a story of one brand's determination to embrace the customer of the future while holding onto a rich legacy of passionate and devoted customers. Now spanning three decades, Tasti D-Lite has not only navigated two different business models within rapidly shifting competitive and economic landscapes, but it has jumped headlong into that great disruption called the Internet and the new frontier that is social media.

You'll find that this book is about breaking free of organizational traditions and conventional approaches, but there is a human case study here as well. While we explore technology and the humanization of brands, the underlying issues will cut to the heart of business and ultimately to the heart of people. Some will find this open future liberating; others will not like what is revealed and may fight it and try to escape its implications. We hope to demonstrate the remarkable power that these new media can have when fanatical customers are engaged through the creative use of social technologies and when transparency is embraced within an organization.

Those familiar with Tasti D-Lite's avant-garde approach to social media and customer loyalty may be expecting us to write about the development and application of these innovative tools. While we address this, we go beyond to the real opportunities and challenges with which we are all faced—to the kind of human innovation that creates a deeper connection with consumers beyond what the gadgets and applications of the day can offer.

Just how did Tasti D-Lite go from an apartment in Manhattan to somehow "become the poster child for online engagement in the franchise world"?[1]

We invite you to read on.

CHAPTER 1

Introduction to a Tasti Story

> The power of social media is it forces necessary change.
>
> —*Erik Qualman, author,* Socialnomics: How Social Media Transforms the Way We Live and Do Business

Tasti D-Lite's core product formulation was developed in 1987 in New York City in the Upper East Side kitchen of Celeste Carlesimo. Seeking to fulfill the changing dietary needs and tastes of New Yorkers, Celeste and her food scientist father Louis created this healthier dairy-based soft-serve version of ice cream that would eventually expand into an offering that would include over 100 flavors as well as line extensions for smoothies, shakes, and sundaes.

Without the butter fat content to properly categorize it as ice cream and no active cultures to call most of the flavors frozen yogurt, the "What is it?" question has always been a curiosity for those feeling the need for a formal classification. For those who have made the short journey from suspicion to obsession, "Tasti D" or simply "Tasti" has become sufficient. For them the question has become, "Where can I get more of it?" Capturing this sentiment online has been fascinating to watch.

Anne Treasure
@annetreasure

Today I had tasti-d-lite for the first time. Peanut butter fudge. My life will never be the same.

New believer: Anne shares her first experience.

Emerging from the first round of fro-yo wars in the late 1980s, robust organic growth through the 1990s, and the start of the new century found Tasti D-Lite being served in some 90 different outlets primarily in the New York City borough of Manhattan. As demand for the product grew, Tasti D-Lite was often bolted onto existing concepts and businesses with names such as Candy Club, Igloo Café, Frozen Monkey, and Sweet City. Most of the outlets at this point were licensed distributors of the product, and Tasti D-Lite could be found within candy shops, alongside magazine stands and even at the back of a furniture store.

The popularity of the frozen treat and signature blue cup became firmly rooted as a staple within Manhattan's culture and would ultimately overflow into television and other media.

In 2004, several episodes of HBO's hit series *Sex and the City* featured unsolicited appearances of the product, which only spread the status and appeal to a wider audience, many members of which were a match for the shape conscious brand demographic. Mentions and appearances continued on shows like *The Apprentice* and *30 Rock* as well as an appearance on the big screen in 2011 in the movie *Our Idiot Brother* starring Paul Rudd and Elizabeth Banks. Another unsolicited cameo in the NBC show *30 Rock* came early in 2012 followed by appearances on the HBO series *Girls*. When stars like Tina Fey initiate these kinds of appearances, the mystique and appeal continues to validate and feed the interest in Tasti D-Lite.

Kara Schmiemeier
@miss_karababy

I wanna go to the tasti d lite here solely for the reason it was on sex and the city! #charlotteandharry

Sex and the City: For many, appearances on television create interest in Tasti D-Lite.

Celebrity appeal aside, it's always been about the love of the product for the faithful. The deep affection found within the core customer base has resulted in remarkable word-of-mouth publicity which continues to drive brand awareness.

Embrace these fanatical customers on the web, and you've got yourself a story. This story.

Crossroads

In 2007, the Tasti D-Lite concept and formula were sold to the New York-based private equity group SPG Partners consisting of Ian Snow, Ogden Phipps, Sean Epps, with Jim Amos as operating partner, chairman, and CEO. Franchising would become the future of Tasti D-Lite with growth plans that included international expansion. A dream team of seasoned industry veterans was assembled. Members of this group have over 250 collective years of franchise experience. Most within this handpicked group had worked together for many years on other concepts. What existed of the small corporate office in New York was relocated to the unlikely city of Franklin, Tennessee, just south of Nashville, where the new Tasti D-Lite infrastructure and leadership began to take shape.

At the point that the concept was acquired, Tasti D-Lite found itself at a crossroads of brand renewal and transition just as social media was starting to hit critical mass. Without robust operational, marketing, technology, and distribution resources in the original business model, the shifting competitive environment and recession of 2008–2009 would soon have an impact on the original outlets in New York City. Putting these resources in place as soon as possible would be critical for not only sustaining but growing the concept.

Meanwhile, a facelift was in order for the 20-year-old aging brand, and a new logo, store design, website, and marketing standards were developed. Continuing to forge a new segment in the frozen dessert industry would mean staying relevant to the needs of the market.

With so many fans familiar with Tasti from time spent in New York, seeds of customers are still lying dormant around the world yearning for their beloved product. Maintaining connections with those both within and now outside the area would be essential for spreading the word later when it came time to launch into new markets, including those overseas.

@Eva4Eva
Eva Bojtos

@tastidlite when are you coming to London? I haven't had a tastidlite since the summer of 2007.

London?: Seeds of customers are spread around the globe.

In a July 2008 article titled "Tasti D-Lite Banks on Its Fanatical Fans for Growth," the *Wall Street Journal* reported it this way, "The chain's biggest challenge may be simply translating a distinctly New York phenomenon to the rest of the country and international markets."[1]

Speed to market was imperative while simultaneously dealing with the massive influx of new fro-yo concepts moving in from the West Coast. At the same time, building an operational engine that would support new locations not only in other areas of the country but in other parts of the world could come only through franchising.

Chief operating officer Peter Holt has been leading the charge since the earliest days of the acquisition. He recalls the operating model at the time, "With so many points of distribution that existed when we acquired the company, what you had was a hundred different versions of what Tasti D-Lite was. Franchising was the most powerful vehicle to accelerate the growth and to develop the brand that so many were wanting to see expand. The standardized systems and infrastructure to support the concept outside of New York had to be put in place as quickly as possible to meet the demand." Continuing to develop the brand would start by having the right operating model.

Keeping the legacy alive while refreshing the brand image with some level of standardization would be the challenge. Also, fostering customer relationships through changing times and business models would be required to extend the vision and dream of what Tasti D-Lite was and what it could be.

Too Much History

Is it possible to have too much history and brand baggage? The multidecade experience of some Tasti customers has painted an interesting picture and perspective of the brand. Most recall the golden years of Tasti D-Lite as those early days of dominance in Manhattan where little competition existed and cult status reigned. But those years were not without controversy.

In 2002, concerns were raised about the accuracy of the nutritional claims of the product by the *New York Times* and later by the New York City Department of Consumer Affairs. The lack of corporate structure as well as little marketing and operational support for the chain made it vulnerable to such claims.[2]

The issue was resolved with the Department of Consumer Affairs by the company implementing an aggressive compliance program with its licensees that focused on serving the customer the proper size (and not overportioning) and ensuring that the soft-serve machine was set up properly to deliver the product with correct density, which influences the caloric value of the product.

For many, this is reminiscent of the *Seinfeld* episode in which suspicions arose over the fat content of the popular frozen yogurt shops of the day. While not directly related, the association remains for many people, even years later.

lyneka little
@lyneka

According to an episode of Seinfeld Tasti d Lite has zero calories. If anyone says otherwise I believe you hate yourself.

Zero calories?: The perception remains, years later.

Too Little History

While the *Sex and the City* and other appearances in TV shows and movies certainly bring some level of awareness and curiosity, that, "What is it?" question still remains for many. The trend and pursuit of healthier living has many people asking questions about everything they eat, and frozen desserts are no exception. While the question needs to be addressed, Tasti D-Lite was not built through converting the skeptics with rational arguments. They just have to taste it. For those who have never experienced Tasti D-Lite, the opportunity is to take them on that head-to-heart journey by simply by getting the product into their hands and mouths.

Providing information on product and flavor offerings became a priority when the product was launched into new markets. Here, social media would also have a role in meeting the needs of the business by establishing and supporting a foundation of trust in order to foster customer loyalty.

Would the product be able to stand on its own and support the concept in new markets where there was little or no brand equity? Throw in a crowded field of upstarts saturating markets with the latest frozen fad of the month in what is considered as the second round of fro-yo wars. The first round occurred in the late 1980s. When asked about those early years, founder Celeste Carlesimo said, "Many other people came out with products that looked the same but really didn't taste right. When it came down to it, it was the taste that made us number one."

Going forward, we knew that the brand would need to stand on three things: taste, health, and the customer experience. These would be the legs of the stool that everything would need to stand on. For example, as we looked at new products to expand the Tasti D-Lite offering, each would need to pass the taste test. Tasti comes first. Each of these elements would have its own role and opportunity as the concept was taken out of New York City.

Opening the Franchise Floodgates

Franchise development manager Kim Falcone remembers when the franchise opportunity opened up in 2008. "I was there when we were going through all the inquiries from years past from people that wanted to open a Tasti D-Lite. They would mail in letters and include pictures of their families on vacation in front of a store in New York."

Reconnecting with those who were at one time interested in franchise ownership gave us a base to work from which would ultimately lead to commitments to open more than 300 locations globally in the coming years.

The next generation of operators is shaping up a little differently. On this subject, Kim shares, "I think the social media is attracting a younger franchise community. People will call in and it's their children that are the fanatics that have interacted with us online and have driven their parents to call and inquire about a franchise."

Traditionally, franchising has grown from candidates who would invest 10 to 20 percent in their businesses and borrow the remainder. Since October 2008, traditional financing has not been available. With local bank lenders requiring as much as 40 percent down and home equity for the remainder, more than half of transactions that can be financed have not occurred. All franchising companies have been seeking innovative ways to continue to develop and grow their networks. In the face of this reality, Tasti D-Lite moved from an organic growth model to a multiple store owner, area developer, international master franchise and nontraditional developer strategy. The franchise candidates have had operational infrastructure experience and were able to self-finance, which is a testimony to the power of the brand.

Georgina Crawford found Tasti in 2003 when she was living in New York City. "I hadn't heard of the brand before, so when I moved into my first apartment in Manhattan and found one around the corner I thought I had discovered the 'next best new thing.' To my surprise, Tasti D-Lite had been around for years and almost every female in Manhattan had already discovered it!" Sometimes discoveries move from a consumer interest to an entrepreneurial interest. Her father John tells the rest of the story; "Several years later, the whole family was based and working in London and we were planning our return to Melbourne after a 20 year absence from Australia. It was then that the we discovered there was a gap in the market for a great tasting, guilt-free frozen dessert, with lower fats, carbs and sugars than traditional ice creams, gelato and frozen yoghurt. In 2010 we commenced negotiations with Tasti D-Lite in the US to acquire the Master Franchise rights for Australia. At this time I was delighted when my son, Jeremy who was then a performing rights and music-publishing executive in London, decided to join the venture. So it's a family affair. Georgina takes responsibility as Director of Marketing and Operations and Jeremy as Director of Business Development." With a corporate flagship already open in Melbourne, the Crawfords opened their first franchised location in Australia in 2012.

In the next chapter we discuss the franchise advantage at greater length.

A Tasti-er Planet

Part of a franchisor's responsibility is to grow the system. When many companies were hunkering down, cutting back, and closing their doors in the faltering economy, 2011 saw a record number of new Tasti D-Lite locations open at a time when much larger concepts grew at a slower rate on a base of thousands of units. Growth through the strategic acquisition of other concepts also became a reality through the purchase of the Planet Smoothie franchise system.

We found the synergies between these two brands to be remarkable. Also the complementary demographic, product mix, nutritional profiles, and market position were a clear fit. More access points in the marketplace would provide both brands the ability to grow and cross-pollinate similar product lines and elevate unit economics throughout the entire system. A marriage of the two concepts would allow us to reach a larger audience.

Just five days after the acquisition was finalized, the marriage was codified at the annual Planet Smoothie conference in Atlanta in December 2011. The energy and dynamic at that first event confirmed the findings from the due diligence process that this was another vibrant brand poised for renewal and growth. Along with a fanatical customer base, the high caliber of franchisees had carried the brand since its birth in 1995.

Planet Smoothie came along more than a year after we started this book project. You'll see a number of mentions throughout as many of the principles followed in its development have application here. Here we are discovering and interacting with a whole new base of loyal customers. While "Planet Tasti" is a term we use to reference the corporate umbrella over both brands, each remains unique and distinct, even when colocated in the same retail space.

Social Negligence

Early in the Tasti D-Lite acquisition process, we started to take a serious look at the content customers were creating on the web around the Tasti D-Lite brand and the product itself. At this point, there was little if any official presence or online engagement from the corporate office. An archaic and relatively static website served as the lone virtual representation of the brand. We found it fascinating however that loyal customers had been busy on their own creating various blogs, groups, pages, and forums related to their Tasti experience. Aside from the periodic contributions of the usual media outlets, people were actively sharing their love for the product with friends within their social networks. Photos on Flickr, reviews on Yelp, and groups on Facebook with names like "Tasti D Lite Addicts" existed for fans to connect to. In hindsight, it would seem logical that such loyalists would spread the word online as they had done organically on the streets of New York City for many years.

We found this description on the "Tasti D Rules My Life" Facebook group: "For all of you New Yorkers out there, you understand the magic of Tasti-D-Lite. Have you ever intentionally ridden the subway 80 blocks to find a particular Tasti location? Tracked down your proximity to a storefront by observing those bright blue cups in garbage cans? Considered and/or have attempted to live solely on Tasti? I don't blame you."[3]

When customers make up their own rules about a how other customers should act around a product, you might be onto something. The 2006 blog post of one enthusiast came up with the "Gospel of Tasti D-Lite" which was a list of admonitions for other customers patiently waiting in line for their Tasti D-Lite.

For example, "If the line at Tasti D-Lite exceeds five (5) persons, you are no longer entitled to a sample."[4]

And what would possess someone to create an entire blog reviewing Tasti D-Lite flavors and products? We discovered one site because of its relatively high search engine ranking which was likely the result of its detailed entries describing and rating each flavor, often including pictures. This was the work of Sam D, a then Yale student and self-described "Tasti D enthusiast/evangelist" who began the blog in August 2007. His fair and honest assessments and commentary were probably the best collection of Tasti D-Lite flavor and product reviews in existence at the time.

His creative four-star flavor rating system was published as follows:

Four stars: D-Liteful
Three stars: Tasti
Two stars: D-List
One star: Nasti

The description of his blog reads: "As my visits to Tasti D-Lite became increasingly frequent, I realized what kept me coming back was the excitement and intrigue that comes with the flavors of the day. Why every flavor looks like chocolate or vanilla is as much a mystery to me as it is to you, but this blog aims to serve as a repository for reviews on and pictures of each Tasti flavor—enjoy!"

The commentary found in the "state of the Tasti" category of posts provides an interesting perspective on changes that were being made during the initial brand transition in 2008. Sam D's comprehensive coverage includes fair and honest comments on the rebranding, online activities, competitors, and franchising. In one post, Sam wrote: "I like to imagine that until the moment I step into the store, the flavors of the day have yet to be decided, and as I push the door open, the frozen dessert gods scan my soul and offer flavors as some sort of karmic redemption."[5]

As excited as we were to find such great content and valuable insights, the harsh reality was that we were neglecting to engage and take advantage of the opportunity to interact, inform, and provide a great online experience.

So it was here that our online adventure began. Our desire to not only recognize these enthusiasts but to build systems and applications to reward them for their digital activity would lead to some exciting days ahead.

Joining the Conversation

While customers don't really need a corporate presence to interact around a product, the undeniable opportunity to be part of the conversation exists for just about any business type. Neglecting that opportunity can be perilous as competitors move in and look for ways to address the unmet needs of consumers in these growing social spaces.

Advances in technology are causing a fundamental shift in customer expectations, behavior, and ultimately control over their marketplace experience. As a result, businesses everywhere are clamoring to get their arms around the image, culture, and experience they deliver online and offline as the greatest transformation in the history of customer relations is now taking place.

This confluence of customer control and corporate transparency is blurring the lines of traditional marketing and revealing the life, culture, and humanity within and around the brands with which we identify.

What will separate the winners from the losers in this new digital age? It will come down to the ability of businesses and organizations to not just allow but embrace transparency and boldly yet humbly meet customers face-to-face in ways previously unseen. Those that are understanding of the opportunity and are changing the way they do business are taking an early lead. As you'll see, there are no shortcuts as search algorithms and social platforms are now rewarding more relevant and authentic advertisers.

Staying ahead in the race for transparency requires a bold vision, a fresh approach, a few geeks, and a heart to help people. There are others working hard to lead the way, helping to break new ground, and setting the pace and parameters for this race. The business case and real-life stories within these pages will challenge the models and mindsets of those with old ways of thinking and inspire new ways of doing business in this digital age of transparency and the humanization of brands. Many other books have defined transparency; this one demonstrates it. Our hope is that this book will inspire the next generation of customer engagement and experience innovators.

At the core of this shift is our longing for connectivity, which is being fed by these new social networks but is ultimately driven by the desire for relationships. We want to share and connect. Caught in the middle are the products and services we use and love, while on the sidelines businesses are battling for fans, followers, and, in the end, loyalty throughout this new media frontier.

A Word About Strategy

Consumer adoption of new technologies has outpaced the ability of businesses and organizations to implement them. Keeping your corporate head above this groundswell of innovation requires just as much vision as it does strategy.

As you'll see, strategy starts with listening. Call it analysis, evaluation, or assessment if you like, but it is all about the least-used tool in the corporate toolbox—listening. More on that in Chapter 4, "Character in 140 Characters."

Having associates that are just as informed about these technologies as customers are is just part of the equation. Many businesses now have two kinds of doors. There's a physical door and a cyber door. With many more people now coming through the latter, there needs to be a consistent experience both virtually and physically. Delivering those human experiences is going to require some emotional energy. Out of this humanness comes something that is reflective of the purpose, the culture, the mission, and values that all contribute to the personality of the brand. People want to be around whom they like and trust. Likability is more of a factor than ever before. There are hard costs associated with brick-and-mortar training, operations, and other disciplines but personality is free. Bad personalities and the poor customer experiences they provide can destroy everything else.

This is easier than it sounds. Having your people and platforms ready is a big part of being in the right position at the right time. Being ready when a new technology comes along is a critical element of any social media strategy.

How do you plan and budget for what does not yet exist and may come and go before you even have a chance to adopt it? It seems that every week new communities or applications emerge that bring with them opportunities for brands to engage.

As we write this, Instagram (acquired by Facebook in 2012) and Pinterest are two that we could name, but where will they be when this book hits the shelves? If you can't see them coming, you'll need to know your customer, the specific needs of the market, and the trends and behaviors that are driving the use of these new technologies.

In hindsight, the presence or lack of strategy and/or preparedness for technology-based innovation is obvious. Milestones that may or may not have been distinct goals in the beginning now become clear. Looking back, we also see those who partnered with us to help us achieve our goals. Investing in the right relationships is a big part of preparedness.

Our acceleration of technological progress has us learning things faster than ever. The momentum of this intellectual runaway carries us to the next idea, iteration, and hopefully success or at least progress, assuming that we come to grips with failing and learning fast. Some are taking risks and riding waves, while many others remain spectators and are just waiting to see if the water is safe. Our argument here would be that being a spectator is no longer safe.

In hard times, thinking "now" versus thinking "big" has many businesses implementing what works today in order to simply make it to tomorrow. When time is of the essence, building things right for the long term has to be carefully balanced with the immediate needs of the business. On one hand, you don't have to worry about scalability in five years if you don't make it to that point. On the other hand, building things to last is just as critical. This is where the start-up entrepreneurial mindset meets and often clashes with the systems and process-oriented thinkers. Both are vital and will have to coexist in organizations that are going to thrive in today's economy.

In times of plenty, customer innovation is likely to get put on the back burner. Many of the stories and examples you'll find here were born not out of a period of surplus, but out of a need to sustain. Necessity is the mother of invention after all. Being relevant is one thing. Staying viable is another. This kind of need brings new discoveries that feed new opportunities, but you have to be in the game to win.

Why This Book?

Various sections in this book outline how certain concepts can be activated in other businesses.

Why on earth would we do that? Is this really an appropriate thing to do in today's cutthroat competitive environment? What about the mindset that says that we have to protect our intellectual property at all costs? Of course there are things that would not be appropriate to share. You won't find within these pages trade secrets like our proprietary formulas and recipes for Tasti D-Lite and Planet Smoothie products.

Increasingly, the value of the intellectual property within an organization exists within the culture it possesses. At one time the argument may have been different. Technology and social media have changed the playing field in such a way that your shiny new asset is just one reverse engineering project away from being replicated elsewhere and then shared virally for free all over the Internet. The business model you create today is likely to be commoditized or found to be not relevant tomorrow because of the rapidly changing needs of the marketplace. With consumers adapting to the latest platforms much faster than we can implement them, technological leapfrogging is happening at very high frequency.

We believe that the future of business and commerce lies within the ability of companies and organizations to not only embrace open technologies but to open philosophies on a much greater scale than they do now. We think that most companies are unwilling to pay the price of patience, innovation, and capital on a material and human level. Success is not only dependent upon the execution and implementation of these new technologies, but upon developing the culture and attitude to support their adoption within the organization.

In the frozen dessert industry, being world class in taste and health is the cost of entry that only gets you through the door. What happens after that and what really makes the difference is the customer experience and ultimately the value of the culture that has grown and been fostered around the brand.

Beyond the readiness of platforms and the preparation of people, there are the relationships that have to be fostered and managed over the long term. For us, there have been numerous critical investments that have played a big part in our being able to execute when necessary. Technology integration is one thing. Cultural integration is altogether different. Managing those relationships over time goes beyond finding the right solutions. It means an integration of values where mutually beneficial solutions and partnerships have what it takes to drive sustainability across organizations.

The acquisition of Tasti D-Lite in 2007 was not of minor consequence. This was not a simple transfer of a business from one set of hands to another. Scaling a regional concept in pursuit of global brand expansion was going to require some help at a whole new level. The following years would be spent developing partnerships to support areas of distribution, technology, product development, training, marketing, and operations.

You Can't Steal Culture

Funny thing about culture; it grows organically. It cannot be manufactured, copied, or moved. It has to be built and cultivated one person, one franchisee, one relationship, and one business unit at a time. The lowest common denominator is the individual.

You can't transfer culture any more than you can transfer intimacy or trust. Life is a journey built on the relationships you invest in. You can't reverse engineer the dynamic of a culture that has grown organically and the people within it who have come together for a common cause and share a common vision.

What you might find missing from this book is many of our missteps. We don't share all our failures. When it comes to social media, we've thrown a lot of mud on the wall. Our depth of experience is valuable to us as a franchise, and as you can imagine, much of that is based on trial and error.

We realize that others have very different views on this kind of open philosophy. It's been interesting interacting with other brand representatives in various disciplines like mobile, communications, and PR and hearing the perspectives and policies around the sharing of information. The contrast between the tight-vested controllers and the brand journalists is becoming clearer. Here, we have to agree with Annette Simmons. Whoever tells the best story wins.[6]

Sure, there will always be the parasites who do nothing but take from what we and others like us openly share. There are significant differences however between climbing to the top of a mountain and taking a helicopter to the top. Even if you get to the same place, it doesn't mean that you've arrived in the same condition. Shortcuts to a perceived destination will not bring growth in strength, vision, experience, or depth of understanding. The character and discipline that are built and developed in the climb will be required to make the next leg of the journey.

Beyond open-book management, there is open-book life. Who we are, where we are, and where we are going are life questions, not business questions. This is about how we view ourselves, the path we are on, and our purpose.

If you are not willing to share, then your view of life is a zero-sum gain where any increase is at the expense of another in equal proportion. In *Enchantment*, Guy Kawasaki uses an eaters versus bakers analogy. "Eaters think that if they win, you lose, and if you win, they lose. Bakers think that everyone can win with a bigger pie."

Case in point, why would we help develop an innovative concept and instead of hoarding that success become an investor in a new venture that makes the solution available for other businesses? See Chapter 7, "Rolling with the Big Boys."

Even if we told you how to do it, could you precisely replicate it in the same way with better results?

Our initial concern (along with that of our literary agent) was that any attempt at telling the Tasti D-Lite story would sound like a self-serving marketing piece. We knew, however, that this story was a compelling one, and while clearly there would be benefit in sharing it, we hope you'll agree that the journey from social negligence to where we are today is one that anyone could learn from, relate to, and find valuable. These are the stories and concepts that have impacted us, not only as a business but as individuals.

There's a growing contrast in the schools of thought between the conventional tight-vested corporate mindset and what we are seeing growing in effectiveness in the new business economy. Organizations are now looking to provide value beyond their core product or service offering and are seeing results. Anecdotal and indirect as these advantages may be, this differentiation can produce opportunities and results not otherwise available.

But how could a desire to serve and enrich the lives of others including potential competitors possibly benefit an organization? And what do social media and the Internet have to do with this? These are just two of the many questions we answer.

This is both a history book and a future book. Sure, we get to tell our version of the story in the light and perspective that we choose. We're the ones holding the pen. You get to pick up your own pen. Start telling your story and see what happens as you do. Be a creator.

We hope that this book crosses a value threshold for you personally. While we feel that there is much to be gained from the insights we share here, we hope you will be challenged both professionally and personally. The mindset and cultural shift we present here can only come from the heart. Serving and enriching the lives of others is not a corporate strategy. It is a mission and a mindset, a vision and a passion. When does business stop being about being in the lead and start being about serving and enriching the lives of others?

As for the timeliness (and hopefully timelessness) of this book, writing about technology in today's world of rapidly changing and emerging trends and applications can be challenging, to say the least. We reference several different current platforms and concepts, but primarily we write this not so much on the applications themselves but on the application of the concepts that will likely remain with us for some time. Concepts like privacy, location, engagement, trust, and culture. Assuming that we'll see these built into more applications going forward, focusing on the foundational principles will help us be ready for whatever comes next. In the same way, we've intentionally left material in this book that will likely be outdated in the near future if it is not already. All this is part of our journey to capture the hearts of our customers.

This and the next two chapters lay a foundation for what we feel is required for building a social enterprise. These prerequisites for using social media to foster loyalty will prepare you for the following chapters.

Your Guides Through This Story

Watching this story unfold and being able to put it into print has been a remarkable experience. We hope the next section will help provide a little context around our backgrounds as coauthors.

The Vision Guy (About Jim as Told by BJ)

I've heard it said that when you write a book, do it as if you were writing for your mentor. It's not every day that you actually get to write a book with a mentor, and I consider it a great honor to do so here. The truth is I rarely read books before meeting Jim. He's helped me see the great value of reading and is largely responsible for that magnetic draw I feel every time I pass a bookstore.

I don't think Jim realizes just how clueless I was in the earliest days of the Tasti D-Lite acquisition as it relates to the opportunity that existed for us online. His early vision around these things was the catalyst that would help drive our pursuit of becoming a social-friendly brand.

While we are both veterans, Jim's service as a U.S. Marine line officer in two combat tours in Vietnam is quite different from my enlisted service in the relative safety of a Navy destroyer during the first Gulf War. Our professional backgrounds vary as well, but differing perspectives and approaches can meet in the middle quite nicely when values and a vision are shared.

Inducted into the International Franchise Association's Hall of Fame in 2011, Jim and his body of work of almost 30 years in the industry has impacted many lives by helping others pursue their dream of small business ownership.

The Technology Guy (About BJ as Told by Jim)

BJ Emerson was running information technology for a company I acquired in 2004. It has been a fascinating study to watch both the personal and professional development of this young man over the last eight years. Today, I count BJ as a friend and brother and have been extraordinarily fortunate to observe him utilize his many gifts in service to others and as a result be recognized for his brilliance, integrity, and diligence.

As BJ and I complete this work, he has become an award-winning social technology executive, having appeared on CNBC and been quoted in the *New York Times*, Reuters, *Inc. Magazine*, *Entrepreneur*, and *AdAge*, as well as the cover of *Hospitality Technology* magazine.

Now considered a social loyalty pioneer, he led the deployment of the first ever loyalty platform featuring integration with Facebook, Twitter, and foursquare and resulting in a variety of industry awards. BJ was once named in Mashable's top 40 brands on Twitter and the people behind them.

BJ has spearheaded the integration of the Tasti D-Lite brand experience with online communities and was largely responsible for taking the brand from a place of social negligence to what is today a place of social prominence.

As you'll see, you'll be introduced to many others who are interwoven throughout this story and who have been instrumental in our pursuit of a dream and building a legacy.

Thank you for letting us share our journey with you. As you take your own, be sure to document your story. We look forward to reading it.

A FEW NOTES

- The first three chapters of this book lay a foundation for understanding the concepts and lessons in the remaining chapters.
- Throughout this book you'll see the term "associates" replace the standard "employee" designation. Culturally, we believe this an important distinction and want to recognize those who work at Planet Tasti as our most valuable asset. You'll meet many of these valuable associates in later chapters.
- To help with some of the technical as well as "Tasti" terms we'll cover, you'll find a glossary at the end of the book for your reference.

The Heart of the Matter

In our discussions with different publishers, we had the opportunity to write a very different book on social media. It would have been, like so many others, filled with a comprehensive and rational justification for things such as transparent leadership, openness, and the impact of technology on the humanization of brands. While important, our desire here is to inspire change through an emotional connection. In addition to addressing these subjects on some level, we hope to cross a human line; the heart line. Simply filling pages on these topics without touching on the heart of these matters would fall short. Brand building at some point requires people building. We believe the real changes necessary for an organization to become more human have everything to do with the humans inside it. Do we really expect change to happen without a discussion on the human condition? The heart is a messy business, but without a holistic look at the root of these issues, we'll never fully rise to the challenge before us.

In their seminal book *Trust Agents: Using the Web to Build Influence, Improve Reputation, and Earn Trust* (Wiley, 2009), Chris Brogan and Julien Smith write, "In social media, human is the new black. People are the next revolution, and being active on the human-faced Web is your company's best chance to grow its business in the coming years." What is required to be active and effective on the human-faced web however will challenge us to the core. When we get real and human through authentic engagement, our values come to light.

We believe that what is required in today's marketplace is innovation of the heart. If you're ready to consider the heart of the matter, this book is for you. Please do not skip this section in each of the following chapters.

We hope you are challenged not only in your thinking and actions but also in your intent. That comes from the heart. So if you're ready to enter the race for transparency, read on.

CHAPTER 2

The Race for Transparency

There is no persuasiveness more
effectual than the transparency of a
single heart, of a sincere life.
—*J. B. Lightfoot*

The race has begun. Indeed, it started some years ago when the very first blog post or online review was submitted by a consumer about a particular service or product experience. Today's social networks are increasingly empowering customers to have a voice and influence others online. Likewise, these communities are providing brands the opportunities to find and engage customers in ways previously unheard of. The resulting fundamental shift in customer control, expectations, and behavior has sent businesses clamoring to get their arms around the image, culture, and experience they deliver. Simultaneously, the competition is heating up and raising the bar as businesses battle for fans, friends, and followers throughout this new media frontier. What will separate the winners from the losers in this new digital age? It will come down to the ability of brands and companies not just to allow but to embrace transparency and bravely but humbly meet customers face-to-face in new ways. The resulting impact on customer relations is the greatest in recent history. The era of getting away with static or automated content on the web has come to an end. Search engines are changing algorithms to favor real and authentic conversations related to a brand, and local search results have become a greater driver of decisions for consumers.

The Human Edge

The race for transparency is a race for the heart of consumers. It's a race for relationships. Greater connectivity means a greater opportunity to connect, emotionally and otherwise. Through technologies such as mobile and location-based services, consumers are making themselves more vulnerable. Smart marketers are not exploiting this but are drawing the hearts of potential customers. That draw can come only from real engagement that has value.

We're challenging you to think differently about how we market to each other and what approaches are truly effective in business and in life. Technology is enlightening the experience, broadening yet deepening the opportunity for something real to happen around a product or a service—not as corporate versus customer, sell versus buy, but as human beings interacting because of their passions and experiences.

The cultural norm is an "us versus them" mindset with corporate on the offense and consumers on the defense. How did we get in these positions? We dread the hard sell. Answering the door or the phone has become painful. We screen everything we can to protect ourselves and to maintain our privacy and dignity. We even have legislation in place designed to protect us from bad marketers in the form of a National Do Not Call Registry. Now the government is involved in how we are being marketed to. Yet we rejoice over the control we have as consumers online where power is restored to its rightful place. The universe is balanced because now as consumers we not only have the power of choice, but we have an unmoderated voice. Social is no longer the future of consumerism; it is the present state of consumerism.

After reading this book, we want people to think differently about what can be possible when technology and humanity collide—not what you can do with technology but how the desire for relationships is still the driver behind why people want to connect. Technology enables, but it takes people to make a meaningful connection.

Where Virtual and Physical Collide

The virtual and physical realms are coming together with mobile and location-based technologies raising the stakes as more and more information is shared. This level of detail is opening new doors and possibilities for the brand experience. As technology allows us to get more granular with regard to products and services, the people and humanity behind the brands are being unveiled.

The virtual and physical realms are colliding as "check-ins" and geotagging have become commonplace through location-based services on mobile devices. Real-time opportunities for transparency and engagement abound when the very important ingredient of location is added along with interactive gaming elements such as competitions for "mayorships" and earning "badges." These new technologies and applications are adding dimensions that require a full understanding of the context of the conversation and activity within them.

The contest, whatever your reasons or motives for entering, is well underway not only for organizations but for individuals as well. But is it correct to say that the company or individuals with the most conversations wins? What about trust and the experiences we provide? How will each of these lead to transactions or should there be a different goal?

For more than 10 years we've been warned of this shift toward transparency in writings like *The Cluetrain Manifesto* (Perseus Books, 2000), *Groundswell* (Harvard Business Press, 2008), *Trust Agents* (Wiley, 2009), and many others. This book is not only a reminder (or a solemn notice in case you've been under a rock) of the continuing shift, but will hopefully provide a healthy mix of the why and the how to go beyond mere survival. As the waters grow deeper and run much faster, you'll need some principles to navigate them on a corporate level as well as individually.

We know that your motives will be tried and your intentions laid out in the hope that what the future holds is worthwhile. Thriving in these new environments will require not only a new mindset but a journey where the difficult questions are not easily answered. For example, do we really want to help people? Do we care enough to serve them based on a sustainable exchange of meeting needs rather than being solely fixated on generating revenue? The sustainable business model will come through creating satisfied customers by meeting their needs and properly managing long-term relationships. The proper assumption is that there is some kind of exchange being made at every touchpoint. The question to be answered is, what are your motives in the exchange?

Understanding New Roles and Expectations

What level of accountability and engagement are customers looking for within these new communities? With a great number of channels with which to potentially connect, the new expectations encompass more than just decent customer service. Customers crave access and information—relevant and accurate information about the products they love. They are creating entire online groups and networks to share this information and support each other with or without brand participation. While corporate involvement is optional (see Social Negligence in Chapter 1), filling the appropriate role and pursuing openness can be the difference between reaping the benefits of being a social friendly brand and falling by the wayside both online and offline.

WHAT CUSTOMERS EXPECT

- **Full disclosure.** Say who you are, what you need, and what your interests are. The tolerance for anything less including anonymity is quickly becoming unacceptable.
- **Authentic interactions.** People want to connect with people, preferably real people. The levels of trust and accountability that consumers are looking for online (and offline) have never been greater.
- **Relevant and valuable information.** Customers want a glimpse behind the corporate veil. What decisions are being made that affect them? What are the future plans for this service or product? Why did that store close? Why did this policy change?
- **Inclusion.** Customers want to be a part of decision making when it comes to products and services they care about. More on this in Chapter 10, "Meet Your Cocreators."
- **Customer service and support.** Consumers are turning to online channels to get the answers and support they need. Their preferred channels vary widely, so brands need listening mechanisms to get visibility to requests, feedback, and complaints.

Brand Fears

Organizations of all types are feeling the impact of social media. Many are responding with a mix of fear, confusion, and uncertainty, while others are jumping in head first with reckless abandon. Handling criticism, maintaining control, and learning how to respond to the real needs of customers are just a few of the issues businesses have to address. These things are happening regardless of businesses' participation. As a result, the thing they fear the most will happen if they do nothing.

Whenever something new comes along, there's an inherent resistance because what you don't know, you fear. In case you are having a hard time identifying these fears, we'll outline just a few here along with a little dose of reality. More detail is provided in other chapters:

1. **My competitors will get too much information.** Yes, they will. They will have access to the same valuable information that is provided to your customers.
2. **My competition will steal my fans/followers.** As some have said, social media is rapidly becoming the great equalizer. So what are you doing about it? If your product or service is inferior, then you have a problem. At the end of the day, the best offering and greatest experience will come out ahead.
3. **It will be an open forum for customer complaints and criticism and our service and support channels aren't set up for this.** The reality is that consumers are already creating their own forums for complaints and criticism. The question is whether you are going to be part of the conversation.
4. **It takes too much time and resources to manage it all.** Yes, it does. Do it right, and the rewards will be there. Do it wrong, and you will waste time and resources.
5. **We will lose all control.** That's already happened if you are allowing others to write the narrative for you. See item 3.

6. **There is no way to measure ROI.** There are more points of measurement within social media than traditional media. Engineer your campaigns right, and you'll have more data on which to base better marketing decisions.

7. **We don't understand the etiquette or protocols and can't keep up with the latest applications and social networks.** That's because you are not listening and investing in the communities where your customers are interacting. Incidentally, digital citizens have little tolerance when businesses are lazy in this area.

8. **Social media is a productivity killer.** You can either stifle the social activity of your employees or empower the social activity of your employees. We explore this in the next chapter.

9. **This kind of communication has to be run through PR or legal.** Perhaps when PR or legal see what the competition is doing in these areas, you might find some ways to streamline your processes. Putting the cultural and communications framework in place to support these initiatives is not an option. Customers are already communicating your brand to others, and they are not asking permission. See Chapter 7, "Rolling with the Big Boys."

10. **Our industry is highly regulated.** If your customers are online, figure out the rules. They will embrace you, and you'll be a leader in your industry.

11. **Most of our customers are not using social media.** Then this is the time to get in. Even if a small segment is online, is it possible that the valuable insights they offer could be shared by others?

12. **My competitors are already so far ahead that we'll never catch up.** With new social networks emerging on a regular basis, the early bird has several advantages. Missing the boat with one opportunity isn't the end of the world, but you should start preparing your organization for the next one. This is not a fad. It's time to get in. See Chapter 7, "Rolling with the Big Boys."

The Content Revolution

We're seeing an explosion of both connections and conversations online. Technology is supplying the connections, but only humanity can supply the interactions. Beyond that point, technology is solely the enabler or supporter of the exchanges and relationships. Technology is simply allowing a greater number of connections. How we manage that pipeline becomes the opportunity.

For marketers, the race for transparency today means a race to create those connections. If marketing is about influencing customer choice, then it needs to start with connecting, conversing, and building trust. Before we can get to any of these, however, we need content—relevant and quality content.

Our insatiable thirst for news, information, images, video, and the associated interaction has created a content revolution. User-generated content (UGC) has been characterized as "conversational media," as opposed to the "mass media" of the past century.[1] As a result, dependence on news and information has shifted away from the traditional methods and channels.

As consumers, we trust UGC over brand messaging and gravitate toward the experiences and recommendations of others. It's still us versus them after all. So how does a brand earn that trust so that its message has at least some influence in the marketplace? For businesses, just being part of the conversation starts with creating and curating their own content. Earning trust and credibility within these communities may not come without the personal recommendations of others.

Where content leads to conversations and experiences, relationships grows in depth and meaning. Intimacy then develops through mutually beneficial exchanges that will ultimately result in influence. The exchange is not always financial, but it is always a resource or something of value.

The amount of influence that a marketer will have in the future is dependent upon the experience provided in the exchange. The result will be more trust and intimacy, less trust, or the same amount.

Simply put, content becomes the seed of conversations. Relationships lead to access, and intimacy leads to influence. The net value becomes one of trusted relationships.

Two-Way Transparency

Transparency works in two directions. Access to more information has proved to be of interest to consumers as they are getting a glimpse into the culture and people behind a product or service. Simultaneously, the wealth of insights and feedback provided by customer-generated content is of great value for those organizations that choose to access it and use it wisely. In many ways, the race for transparency has also become a race for information. The question has become how fast or effectively can you listen, respond, and change to the needs of the marketplace? With instant access to real-time data through things like surveys, trending topics, and forums, companies are limited only by how well they can absorb, adapt, and execute.

Before jumping into the conversation within the various channels, you need to achieve a certain level of understanding and learning. Each social network has its own etiquette, dynamics, and spirit. Knowing the differences and the accepted methods for interacting will start the credibility ball rolling.

Listen, Listen, and Then Listen Some More

One of the popular questions we've fielded on a regular basis over the years has been, "How do you know where your customers are online?" Furthermore, "How do you know how they will respond to your efforts?" and "How do you know where to invest your time and energy?"

Many social and mobile applications may be closed networks by default but may offer integration with Twitter. In other words, the content created by users is private on the given social network unless users choose to share it out. They can do this by enabling a connection to their Twitter profile which is public by default. A little investigative work will reveal the root applications that were used to generate the content of interest such as a keyword or a brand mention. Each tweet reveals the originating application or other social network that pushed it. Doing some research into what apps (applications) are being used can speak volumes about customers. Are they using mobile devices, or are they desktop clients when they create content? What time of the day do they use each? What new applications or communities are they engaging in that may have opportunities for businesses? While many social networks are based on people, location-based services have physical venues as the core objects. Others are based on events. TV shows and menu items have their own social networks in GetGlue and Foodspotting, respectively.

An entire industry has emerged to meet the needs of the listening business. While tools like Google Alerts are a good place to start, these are merely the top fodder—the low-hanging fruit. While you don't necessarily need to be a part of every conversation, doing so can certainly yield valuable insights into consumer behavior. Understanding the dynamics and context of the conversations is key in listening. Understanding the actual interaction around a product or service will reveal the true pulse and sentiment of the consumer. Measuring this sentiment can be tricky, but the technology for doing so is rapidly evolving to provide more accurate results. Many free services exist that show volume and sentiment for a particular keyword or brand expression.

As much as we all would like to get out from behind our desks and spend more time in a Tasti D-Lite or Planet Smoothie store, being able to capture the virtual insights can sometimes reveal more than actually being there. Customers will share things with their social network that they might not say to someone behind a counter. While there is no replacement for face-to-face communication, we'll explain how and why keeping an eye on the social radar is just good business.

Jumping In with Both Ears

Jumping into the realm of social media can be a daunting venture for any business. Jenny Dervin is vice president of corporate communications for JetBlue Airways. JetBlue was another early brand to navigate networks like Twitter and Facebook. When it comes to brand fears and listening, Jenny says, "I have to assume that people who are resistant to understanding how the marketplace is actually talking about a brand are resistant because they don't want to be obligated to act on things that are going on. When you are hit in the face with how people are actually talking about your business and it's not nice, then either you act or leave. It's the classic fight or flight response."

In our case, diving in and engaging fanatical customers that were already "mashing up" a brand name without us was a little bit of a white-knuckle experience. How would the community respond when a corporate presence tried to get in on the action? Engaging without disturbing the organic ambience requires some discernment around site etiquette and the effective use of the best tool of all; big ears. We spent several months simply listening (reading) on sites like Twitter and Facebook to understand the opportunities, and more important, how to participate within the spirit of these communities. We were delighted to find that our approach and presence were welcomed with open arms. How do customers feel when a brand "follows" them? Here's just a sampling of what we see on a regular basis:

"Whoa, @tastidlite is now following me on Twitter. That's like second base."

"After I mentioned them, @tastidlite is now following me on here! Sweet."

"I don't know what's better, @heidimontag following me, or @tastidlite . . . !"

"My life is complete. @PlanetSmoothie now follows me! Someday I will own a franchise!"

With the wealth of information now available online, getting visibility is critical. There are a wide range of applications that are available to meet the listening needs of businesses both large and small. Some are free, but enterprise-level monitoring platforms also exist with features like robust dashboards, alerts, and comprehensive reports. Literally any size business can set up mechanisms for listening online.

When vice president of marketing, Donna Smith, joined us in late 2011, she jumped in with both ears and was pleasantly surprised at what she found. "As a marketer, it is vital to understand the impact of your brand and your promotions on the consumer. Typically we would need to wait until the promotion or campaign was well underway before we could garner any insights or get access to the metrics. With the social media tools we have been using, we are able to get real-time responses on how effective our efforts are and how consumers are perceiving the brand. As a result, we are able to make faster and more relevant decisions to better meet the needs of our customers."

Once the listening is in place, the opportunities that present themselves for engagement will become clear.

The Time Element

In many races, the clock can be as much of an adversary as the opponent. Response time has become a critical factor in the race for transparency regardless of whether or not a competitor is involved.

The day is here when the smart competitor is proactively pursuing the disgruntled consumer. What if a customer complains about a product or service in a public forum and a competitor is the first to respond with an invitation or some kind of offer to meet the customer's needs? What if misinformation goes viral because of a lack of response? This is already happening.

Customers have come to expect real-time response and engagement, not something scrubbed free of reality, spun through marketing or PR, and filled with fine print or disclaimers. They are typically fair and realistic, but above all they want a real human response empowered with the authority to solve problems within a reasonable amount of time.

While the technology exists to monitor and even automatically respond when brand mentions are posted online, only an authentic reply with a personal touch will come out ahead. Sending a letter to arrive weeks or even days later may no longer be effective. Customers expect real-time responses and resolutions, and the window of opportunity to address a concern is limited. How long it takes to respond can be just as critical as the content and spirit of the reply. Inaccurate or misinformation can spread rapidly in the time it takes to effectively respond to a consumer post. Done in short order the correct way, conversations can be turned from potentially negative buzz into a learning moment that reaches many customers.

The challenge then becomes the business's ability to deliver the right content at the right time. In many organizations, certain responses have to be filtered through various departments including legal, marketing, or PR. That archive of preapproved, copied, and pasted responses may address some of the needs, but the vast majority are going to require a quick thinker who knows the business and who is empowered to share it in the right voice. More on this in Chapter 6, "You Can't Outsource Relationships."

The Most Powerful Word on the Internet

Beyond having big ears, do first responders have the edge? The race can be a pursuit of opportunity when it comes to catching consumers in the midst of a purchase decision. One of our favorite examples of this in real time is an exchange that took place in April of 2009 when the following was posted on Twitter by Lauren (@paperelle):

Lauren
@paperelle

waiting for 4:30. Going uptown to meet husband to get some tasti d-lite or Mr. Softee, then dinner with friends. Mmmm…ice cream…

Waiting: Lauren shares the who, what, when, where, and why of her plans.

Following someone on Twitter will normally trigger a notification e-mail to the user. In this case, we were monitoring the term Tasti D-Lite, and we followed Lauren just to let her know we were listening. Just 12 minutes after her initial tweet, she posted:

Lauren
@paperelle

OMG, @tastidlite is now following me on Twitter! Quick, where's Mr. Softee?!

OMG: Will the competitor respond? Is someone there even listening?

The remainder of the conversation was shared via direct message and is shared here with permission:

@tastidlite
Tasti D-Lite

Not sure you will find them twittering from their trucks… How about a coupon? What location you headed to?

Lauren
@paperelle

True, true. Thanks, I followed some of you previous tweets and found the val-pak coupons. I got a yummy brownie batter cone, thank you!

Brownie Batter: Lauren was actually ahead of us this time.

What's the most important word? It was not our search term but what came after it that held the real opportunity in this case. That simple "or" found in between two (or more) names raises the stakes as the potential customer has yet to make up her mind. Meeting her at the right time can make the all the difference. Note however that the valuable information we had posted prior to this encounter set the hook but more on creating engaging content later.

Social CRM

Social CRM (customer relationship management) touches customers where they live on the social web. Beyond storing the typical contact information, social CRM can include social media identities like Twitter, Facebook, LinkedIn, and others. Identifying and keeping in touch with a Tasti brand advocate in a particular area, for example, could be one use of social CRM. Traditional CRM solutions have already started to build these kinds of social tentacles into their software. Low-budget versions exist for those who want to start a database of this sort.

Investing in social networks that have a global footprint opens up social CRM opportunities on a scale previously unheard of. Now critical for brand expansion, seed planting within these communities can make for some interesting prospects and long-term relationships in new markets. As we mentioned, holding onto the hearts of core Tasti D-Lite customers now outside of New York City would be essential for expansion.

The single most common inquiry we receive online is, "When are you coming to _____?" As New York area residents or visitors spread out across the globe, those key connections become valuable touch points that can unlock networks of like-minded consumers.

@ohmypuddin
Lauren W. Madrid

@tastidlite are there plans to open a tasti d-lite in san antonio, tx?

Plans?: Many inquiries have to do with opening in new cities.

As these connections lead to conversations, we often ask for some input on where to open a new location. We can then pass the feedback along to the new franchise owners when the time comes. Meanwhile, the fan and follower mechanisms create that first critical link toward a new relationship.

@donstugots
DonStugots

@tastidlite anything in the tampa area?

@tastidlite
Tasti D-Lite

@donstugots looking for space now, what area do you recommend?

Tampa?: Some customers offer ideas about where to open new franchises.

The more conversation there is within a community, the more potential exposure there is to curious friends not familiar with Tasti D-Lite.

Crossing the Line

Extending the customer relationship online can be fun and engaging, but it's still a virtual relationship. You can't shake hands or exchange a smile. Bridging the gap between the virtual and physical realms starts with a real connection of some sort. Stepping across that line is a little awkward. Customers cross the line when they step foot in a store, but interesting things can happen when the line is breached in the other direction, and there's a proactive and unexpected visit from the other side.

Simple online campaigns and promotions can lead to bigger face-to-face opportunities. Follower contests on Twitter allow us to not only attract new followers, but create lasting touch points with new advocates if we can provide a great experience.

One example comes through the follower challenge on Twitter. As a new milestone is reached in the follower count, the promotion begins with messages like this:

Tasti D-Lite
@tastidlite

Follower #500 gets a $25 TreatCard http://bit.ly/Fpki6 Will it be one of your friends? (Assuming they will share.)

Follower challenge: Gift cards are awarded to the follower who hits the magic number.

The hope here is that current followers of the account will share the information with others through retweets or simply by word of mouth. The friend who happens to hit the magic number when he or she follows becomes the winner. Hopefully the winner will share the winnings with the friend who made the referral.

In New York, entire offices have been known to conspire to win the coveted prizes. We've heard reports of people not wanting to go to lunch so that everyone can follow at just the right time to push the number over the top. It doesn't necessarily matter who the winner is just as long as everyone in the office gets to share the bounty.

Taking this kind of contest to the next level doesn't require much creativity, especially when there is a place of business involved. Simply mailing the TreatCard to the winner would certainly be acceptable, but it would be rather lame in our opinion. A little boldness and resourcefulness could extend a gesture of appreciation and perhaps create a way to make a greater and more lasting impact.

In the case above, follower number 500 was actually a business account for Patron Technology (@patrontcs) managed, of course, by a real person named Chelsea (@seajo).

After requesting the address, members of our local staff took it upon themselves to not only hand deliver the TreatCard, but to bring a Tasti D-Lite cake and some other frozen treats to the Patron Technology office unannounced. Below is Chelsea with the cake and the office party that was held to celebrate the win.

Patrontcs
@patrontcs

PT's offices just got greeted by @tastidlite for a cake and gift card-- so exciting! Thanks, @tastidlite!

So exciting!: The winner talks about the surprise visit.

Thumbs up: The winners have a party with their Tasti treats.

The prospect of bridging the gap between online activity and physical connection is limited only by one's imagination. As brands get more confident (and more competitive), we will see more creative uses of offline campaigns based on virtual activity.

The Hole Shot

In certain dirtbike racing competitions, the "hole shot" is the position of the racer at the front of the pack when approaching the first sharp turn after the initial straightaway. In other words, when a group of competitors comes off the line at the same time, the single rider to break free and get to the first corner has emerged unencumbered by the pack which is forced to make the turn together. It is at this turn that the group faces the greatest risk of colliding and stumbling over each other with disastrous results. The leader has the advantage as he or she cleanly navigates the turn and can focus on what is ahead instead of muddling through a crowded landscape of competitors.

The same concept applies to pursuing transparency on the web. Those early brands that have emerged online to engage and embrace their customers are earning valuable word-of-mouth endorsements, credibility, and press.

Perhaps a Wild West analogy would paint a better picture. The wagon trains have long since left. The great rush to get online is well under way, and the pioneers are staking their claims. Are the leaders sometimes the first to get shot? Can we make mistakes and find ourselves in a PR mess? Of course. The Wild West wasn't for the cowardly and neither is this. There will be casualties, but we are all faced with finding new ways to do business. The gold is out there, so let's get on with it.

The business cycle of entrepreneurship, growth, decline, and renewal was the same in the past as it is today. The only difference is that it is compressed so that businesses have to stay in a constant state of renewal or they lose. As with other times in history, some will adapt and others won't. There will always be stronger people and weaker people, leaders and followers, but the leaders bring along with them those who were afraid to start. What lays ahead for everyone is the promise of increased efficiency, convenience, and the ability to solve problems for customers and businesses.

The Franchise Advantage

The impact of social media has been of particular concern to franchise systems. At the store level, new social and mobile applications are disrupting traditional local marketing models. What used to be a very simple part of owning a local business has many people struggling to keep up with the latest advertising platforms. With so many avenues to reach the target market, the combinations for success are more complicated than ever.

Historically, there have been two general perspectives on franchise brand management. Varying degrees exist, but one end of the spectrum finds heavy-handed control, and the other end features an empowered network of local owners providing unique customer experiences. Commitment to perfect duplication and operational efficiency has been the hallmark of business format franchising. One of the macro trends resulting from our global economic issues as well as the impact of social media is greater flexibility in franchising operating models. What remains is strong adherence to things like branding, products and services. Everything else remains open for discussion.

At the franchisor level, the death of standardization and the rise of personalization mean that more consideration needs to be given to the local brand presence. This comes in the form of tools and resources brought to the unit level where the customers are interacting. Without these, a franchisee is paralyzed.

One problem with this approach is that the relevant content needed at the local level cannot easily be scaled from the top down. Local ownership meets the demand for localized content. Only local and invested ownership can effectively meet those needs at the neighborhood level. Done right, franchising and social media fit quite nicely together. Capturing the local flavor while leveraging the value of a global brand image is a powerful opportunity for franchise organizations.

We're asked on a regular basis how to scale social media efforts. The best thing we can do is equip our network so that franchisees and corporate store managers can reach their local customers where they are online. One example of this for us is local Facebook business pages for each location where community discussions can take place. Centralizing but comanaging other virtual real estate like Google Places and foursquare venues is another way to scale while stewarding the brand assets online.

A white paper distributed by Hearsay Social titled "The Power of Going Local: Comparing the Impact of Corporate Versus Local Facebook Pages" reported that locally created Facebook pages deliver five times more reach, posts provide eight times more fan engagement, and one local fan is worth 40 corporate fans. Craig LeGrande, managing partner of market research firm Mainstay Salire, said, "What the results suggest is that a corporate-based Facebook presence is fine, but that's only the tip of the iceberg. A broader strategy that integrates your corporate Facebook presence with a network of local pages has the potential to drive dramatically greater business results."[2]

When it comes to control, we see many franchisors taking a hard look at existing policies and procedures, and as a result, they are opening up in a spirit of partnership to comanage the brand. Jack Monson is vice president of Engage121, a company that specializes in social CRM and social media management software for the franchise industry. Jack says, "Many more franchise systems are changing the posture from that of control to empowering the system to take advantage of the franchise model. This fits extremely well with the needs of the social consumer."

Jack offers three ways to empower franchisees:

1. Having policies in place will help define relationships and establish guidelines.
2. Training and education will show franchisees how to be good comanagers of the brand while embracing the local audience.
3. Giving them the right tools, content, and controls will help them meet their customers where they are online.

While each location can have a unique voice and provide a personal touch to its online presence, the overall experience is consistent if brand standards are valued and implemented. Legal policies and guidelines are another shared resource that franchisees have access to.

As the curator of the digital content library, the franchisor can serve as the manager and distributor of the social knowledge base. Case studies can help franchisees understand the opportunities within the various social channels and how they might consider running a campaign similar to one done in the past by others.

Steve Caldeira is president and CEO of the International Franchise Association, the world's oldest and largest organization representing the franchising industry. We asked Steve his thoughts on the franchise advantage. "A franchise system can use social media to connect with customers more directly and in rapid response more quickly than any other type of business. And depending on the arrangement between the franchisee and franchisor, the connection can come from the store level locally or from the franchisor at corporate headquarters. All it has to do is listen to what its customers are saying and have the processes in place."

Certain types of businesses are going to have more to deal with than others in industries such as finance when it comes to compliance. In some concepts, approval may need to come through legal; others through marketing or PR. If content is provided in a library, then franchisees have the option to push that to their feed based on local needs. Alternatively, a franchisee creates the content, and there is a review process.

Having a network of similar business units pooling information provides the individual owner with more content to draw on to engage customers. Best practices can be shared as to what works with respect to contests and promotions. COO Peter Holt offers, "Franchising is the business of replication. One of the most powerful things about franchising is the shared learning. Good franchisors continue to monitor that to make sure that you're capturing the experiences that are positive and bringing them back into the network so you can share the impact it can have." Also, if the franchisor can centralize the expertise and provide it to the local franchisee business, it is more likely to be competitive. Independent businesses each have to find those resources on their own, which can be costly.

But this mindset is no different from what existed before the Internet. The mindset of fear and control in a franchisor can manifest itself in many ways including discouraging franchisees from participating in networks like the International Franchise Organization. In fact, for many years, the IFA itself did not embrace franchisees as part of the organization but has since involved them at every level including chairman.

Others with the same mindset are afraid that franchisees will step outside the vendor and buying relationships and find alternative and cheaper sources of products and services. Fearful that somehow they would lose control of their franchise system, the reality is that they have less control now than they have ever had. These are many times good intentions, at least in the mind of the franchisor, but often the opposite is true.

Steve Burnett owns and operates a Tasti D-Lite location in Jacksonville, Florida. As a baby boomer, interacting with customers on Facebook does not come naturally to him, but upon opening his new business, he saw the value and potential it could bring. When asked about his use of social media, he says, "I think it is important for me and other franchise owners to see what is happening online. It kind of gets you outside of the four walls. I need to be there and tend to business, but social media allows me to connect with people without having to leave the shop."

Beyond consumer connections, networking with other local businesses has brought value to his business. Steve continues, "I like to support and interact with local organizations by adding them as favorites to our Facebook business page. I've had them express their appreciation, and that was how they connected; they realized that we were not just some regular ice cream or yogurt shop. When they were looking for dessert vendors, we were top of mind. I would have never connected with them otherwise."

A unique franchise may be an oxymoron to some, but is it the future? Again, business models of all kinds are being challenged.

Whatever those models look like, relevance in the marketplace means having the infrastructure to support authentic relationships with consumers.

Measuring Transparency

For the analytical types, our next point may hurt a bit. Organizational transparency online or offline is not likely to be something you will be able to engineer or fully measure. It's not measurable, at least not in the way that most analysts would prefer it to be or in the way most goal setters and strategic planners would choose it to be.

Just how authentic or real can a business become and to what degree? Can objectives and goals be set for such an endeavor? If so, what are the benchmarks and who decides what they are? Should we pursue new metrics such as key humanness indicators? While that might have some interesting prospects, the very thought of trying to measure such things misses the point. Also, attempting to measure a program can change the very behavior you are trying to measure. The result may lead you to a different outcome from what you set the program in place to begin with.

As the saying goes, "Not everything that counts can be measured. Not everything that can be measured counts."

This Is All Optional, Right?

Many people in the business world are still actively fighting this shift toward authenticity and openness. For them, it is effectively the race for transparency in reverse. The closed mindset says to withhold information, hide behind marketing speak, and put systems and processes in place as fast as possible to support this tight-vested approach. Such businesses are deluded. This mindset reflects constant worry and fear, which is the opposite of forward and positive thinking. Motives, values, and fears aside, sustainability will become the issue for those who are not ready to get human and embrace customers on their terms.

We find this mindset reminiscent of those who took the position in the past that they would not compete internationally. The reality is that you are going to compete globally today whether you want to or not. Likewise, participating in what is happening within today's online communities is not optional. You are in it by proxy. Do you want to be a part of the message, or do want someone else to dictate that message to you? Do you want to be an influencer, or do you not? Congratulations, you're already in the race.

Coming Full Circle

Continuing the racetrack metaphor, those who get out ahead are often the first to come full circle in the cycle of innovation. You see and understand what trends are coming next. You know where the ups and downs or twists and hazards are in the road. There is no cutting in line when it comes to gaining this experience. You can't skip steps. Being an early adopter of social technologies put us ahead of the curve on many of these issues, but, as it turns out, it's really a mindset and heart-set that has made and will make the difference.

Embracing social media has enlarged our business. Perhaps more accurately, it has enlarged the heart of our business. This of course will not guarantee success, but we are quickly approaching a tipping point where not participating in the conversation will guarantee failure. From a process standpoint as well as from a people standpoint, there's much more to explore. Next we take a peek at what's really behind a brand.

The Heart of the Matter

Building a brand customers crave in today's marketplace is going to require a different approach—a human approach. We are making a case here for behavior modification and change toward a result that is beneficial. This call to participate is beneficial only if it is approached with the right mindset and attitude. These cannot come without embracing the right values for the right reasons. There's value not only in participating in the dialogue but also value in participating in a particular way.

Transparency is not possible without a culture and leadership that support and reflect transparency. Those issues and fears impeding openness within an organization will need to be addressed. Removing processes or people may be the challenge for some. Going off-script will be the problem for others.

Leadership in this area means taking the initiative before being forced to act. Writing bigger checks and outsourcing customer relationships will not address the issues at hand. Real leaders will figure out the elements required to create an atmosphere in which culture can grow. Those not able to allow a little cultural autonomy will soon find themselves in a shrinking pool of followers as more attractive options emerge.

All the dynamics of human nature are alive and thriving in this technology world. People and companies are afraid, but businesses have to stay in a constant state of renewal, or they will lose.

As mentioned earlier, following the journey of today's dynamic customer is going to require great flexibility. So who can become more human first? For that question, we need to dig a little deeper and address the building blocks of any organization. Transparency starts at the individual level. Here, a race of personal brand building and of raising social equity is afoot. With Google as your résumé, you have nothing to fear, right?

CHAPTER 3

Going Behind the Brand

> What is REAL? . . . Does it hurt?
> —*The Velveteen Rabbit*

Behind every brand, organization, and government there are individuals. Regardless of the emotional connections consumers may have with a product, the culture and people behind the experience and the product are increasingly judged as part of the brand. Systems and processes don't manage themselves. Embraced or not, the information available on today's web is giving customers a good look into corporate policies, procedures, and ultimately the people making the decisions. Are those who are managing their beloved product worthy of such a responsibility? Is there an openness and willingness to give customers a part in driving the brand experience or does fear and control reign? While fear and control can be collective attributes of any organization, at the end of the day these are individual traits. It is individual traits that reflect either an open mentality or a closed mentality. If closed, individuals and corporations end up building walls around themselves where they cannot get out and others cannot get in.

How does the overall product or service including all the elements factor into driving customer loyalty? Just how important is what or who is behind the brand? Loyalty is based on trust, and the object of that trust is now viewed as an entire package with components being values, people, and overall culture. Loyalty to a product alone goes only so far because it will be replicated elsewhere at a better price, but you cannot commoditize culture. More on this in Chapter 8, "Brand Stewardship."

Do Customers Care?

For years we've seen the professional head shots and bios of executive teams on company websites. These may give us a look at who's behind the veil, but what does it do for us? What do we gain from this kind of transparency? Ultimately, people want to do business with people they like and trust. This transparency is giving us more reasons to choose them over the anonymous competitor, but will that really make a difference? It will if we trust the messages and the messenger.

Increasingly, we are getting to know the people behind the scenes—at least as much as companies want us to see. We don't even have to go online. Look no further than the Domino's "pizza tracker" people or the Red Lobster fishermen we see in commercials. We believe they are real, but are they likable? More important, are they trustworthy? Or are we falling victim to the latest evolution of marketing and PR tactics? In order to trust the message, do we not need to have a messenger we can trust?

With so many options in the marketplace from which to choose, we are forced to find a reason to eliminate or disqualify some choices in order to make a decision. All else being equal, it will be the personal or emotional connection that is going to come out ahead for most humans. If we feel safe, validated, and trusting, we'll choose transparency and effectively disqualify the anonymous.

Someone once said, "It's harder to distrust a person than it is to distrust a corporation." Best Buy CMO Barry Judge has this to offer: "To the extent that we can be human, we will be fostering a deeper level of trust with customers." In Chris Brogan and Julien Smith's *Trust Agents* (Wiley, 2009), we learn all about the influence of those who use the web to build relationships and humanize businesses by applying transparency. It's been said that trust is the new business currency, but only because it is a personal currency, a human currency. The problem is that our default position is distrust, and simply being human doesn't automatically grant us anything. Unless we have validated the relationship through exhibiting the proper values and the proper outlook on life, and unless we are committed to the same things, we won't have a foundation for trust.

We talk about the risks of outsourcing this transparency in Chapter 6, "You Can't Outsource Relationships."

Transparency Is Not My Job

What will happen to those who choose to elude transparency? One result may be that other people will define who they are for them, and the definition may be accurate or inaccurate. As we discuss in Chapter 2, "The Race for Transparency," organizations as a whole are moving toward authenticity and openness. This unveiling will eventually bring to light the individuals behind them. Will these people scatter like cockroaches who seek the safety of the dark? If so, where will they go? There are still plenty of companies where they will fit right in with that old-school tight-vested mindset and culture. These are the individuals and companies that are moving in exactly the wrong direction with fear and control as common denominators. Time is not on their side, and those dark corners are going to become very lonely as fellow employees embrace transparency, and new blood comes into the workforce.

Google Is Your Résumé

Do a Google search for your name. What do you find? Is it good news or bad news? Those who are serious about competing in today's economy are intentionally and systematically developing online profiles, creating relevant content, and setting themselves apart knowing that they are a brand that needs to be managed. Focusing on a certain niche and associated keywords as an individual can help establish you as a thought leader and innovator. With more employers going online to research job candidates, those who are showing their value and expertise through content creation and engagement will stand out above the rest.

However, it will be interesting to see how the tables could get turned if employers are found discriminating against those without online profiles, and claims of "disparate treatment" become an issue during the recruitment process.[1]

Our general counsel Grayson Brown offers this, "The burden of developing guidelines and clear hiring policies related to social media is on the employer to help make the right decisions. This is an area of growth that will continue to change."

Regardless of how employers deal with it, managing a personal brand and reputation online has become a huge opportunity for individuals in most industries.

As we say earlier, without being part of the conversation, others will by default write the narrative for you. Without an algorithm for truth, search engines simply return whatever results offer the best content based on the selected keywords. As we see in Chapter 5, "Don't Be Boring (and Other Thoughts on Relevance)," their job is to provide the most relevant results, and you (and your business) are just another keyword.

Putting your best foot forward on the web means carefully managing your personal brand. These apply to businesses as well as individuals:

1. **Create and curate your own content.** Understand the difference between and value of both earned media and owned media and how to use each effectively. Simply put, earned media are created by others, owned media are created by you. We cover creation and curation in Chapter 8, "Brand Stewardship."
2. **Think like a search engine.** Be specific and intentional when it comes to key words and phrases tied to your name. Your brand is your responsibility.
3. **Start early and monitor often.** If you let things get away from you, you will have that much more to deal with later. Don't let others dictate the search engine results by running away with the conversation.
4. **Don't give them something negative to say.** Know that what you publish will face scrutiny. Be thoughtful about your content and be ready to defend your position.

Finding Value in Transparency

Seeing the value in transparency as an individual is the start of being competitive in this new business environment. This will, however, require an assessment of the core values that lay beneath the transparency.

Deb Evans is a franchise friend, an executive, and a social-savvy grandmother who is no stranger to transparency. On the contrary, her investment in social networking in the last few years has helped her to continue to develop and grow personally as well as professionally. Well known as an advocate for franchising and social media, she offers this:

> Investing the time in social media and building those relationships, for me as an individual, have certainly improved my leadership skills within my organization. There are professionals whom I have been following and communicating with, and building relationships with for the last three years. With social media, it really is social, but you have to build trust. These networks allow you to understand who people are as individuals, and then you learn more about their business philosophy and what services or products they provide. Being able to find those you align with can be of great value.

But is this just a different channel for something you would otherwise do at the Rotary Club or chamber of commerce meeting? How is it different? Deb says "Building relationships in the virtual world is different from IRL [in real life]. It's not as easy to be transparent virtually, but it's a necessity in order to build trust. Social media allows a multichannel, one-to-many approach to building awareness and engagement. In a chamber of commerce or Rotary meeting, you are networking one to one."

If we value relationships, one of the ways to stay connected or to deepen those relationships is to use the new social tools that are available. Those who use these tools will evolve in their thinking more quickly than those who don't because they have more connections and engagement. There are people whom we identify with through common interests and we can learn from them as well as those whom we don't agree with but with whom we can interact.

"Brandividuals"

Founders of businesses and CEOs have historically been the highly visible and recognized representatives of a brand. Recently, however, everyday associates have been stepping into the spotlight and becoming not only ambassadors but in certain cases the face of the brand. One simple definition of a *brandividual* is a real person who helps others trust a company by virtue of his or her humanity.[2]

A brandividual is someone who has, over time, so closely identified himself or herself with a brand name that the two become hard to separate. When you think of one, you think of the other. Jared Fogle from Subway is an early example of a real person sharing an inspiring story that has no doubt impacted many. Watch him holding up the humongous pants he used to wear, and you just got humanized. The emotional connection is there because of the power of his personal testimony.

Another definition of brandividual we found was "an individual employee who draws on her or his personal identity as well as the organization or brand's identity to represent the organization or brand in online relationships."[3]

In the case of Red Lobster, you see a clear push to put faces and job descriptions to those behind the brand. The message will connect much more deeply when it comes from a real behind-the-scenes person and not an actor.

Another good example is the Ford Motor Company. When we think of a paid spokesperson in Ford's television commercials, we think of Mike Rowe. Take a look online however, and the real brandividual you'll find with great influence in the social channels is Scott Monty, Ford's head of social media.

It would seem that these brandividuals are starting to replace the icons that we have known for years such as Ronald McDonald or the king from Burger King, the latter was retired in 2011. It's clear to see that these types of characters are becoming less effective in marketing because our desire is to connect with people, preferably real people.

Some questions remain. Are brandividuals a potential risk to corporations, and what risk is that individual taking? Should individuals try to avoid such an association? What if there is a personal failure? Or a corporate failure?

David Armano, executive vice president of global innovation and integration at Edelman Digital, writes, "As the dawning of the age of the brandividual comes upon us, we'll all have to rethink the boundaries between us as individuals, brands, and the brands who employ us."[4]

Taking Your Relationships with You

Within social networks, the lines between individual and brands can be quite blurry. BBC chief political correspondent Laura Kuenssberg (@BBCLauraK on Twitter) had over 60,000 followers on Twitter in July 2011. She took all of them with her when she became business editor of ITV. A simple Twitter account name change allowed her to become @ITVLauraK, and she was able to retain all her contacts and those she was interacting with.

In another case, Noah Kravitz, who worked at Phonedog. com, managed the Twitter handle @Phonedog_Noah and had a following of 17,000. When he left his job, he became @ NoahKravitz, and all his followers went with him. In this case, the employer ended up filing suit against him for over a quarter of a million dollars to try and get those followers back.[5]

The ownership lines become blurred when brand and individual accounts are mixed unless some clear policies are put in place and the purpose of the account is established before it is created. Policies aside, this is about relationship building and the old-school Rolodex is now on steroids. Understanding the value and potential of these relationships and the influence of individuals will go a long way toward establishing clear employment parameters. In the Phonedog.com case above, one would have to question whether the company really had an appreciation of the importance of this social capital before or even during the time the employee was managing the account. It all goes back to step one—listening.

Staying Competitive in a Digital Age

Members of the next generation are primed for transparency. They have lived and breathed social networking, are accustomed to having immediate access to any online resource, and have lower barriers when it comes to privacy. As these digital natives start to permeate the workforce, the shift toward openness will come from inside out as new employees meet their peer customers who share the same mindset. So how is the mature workforce going to deal with the changing tide? The line between old-school thinkers and the socially astute is becoming clearer. As more companies look to hire for transparency, those who are just learning these skills will be faced with either adapting or being downgraded to second- or third-tier employees and possibly even extinction.

Many new companies have the advantage of hiring and growing this way and are putting the processes in place to do so from day one. The human resources hiring practices have evolved, and the HR gateway is driving the future of the corporate culture with an intention never before seen. These companies of the future have refined their filters for finding the indispensable; those who understand the mindset that says that everyone is in the marketing department, that everyone is in customer service. As a result, the DNA of a transparent organization is made up of the people within who are open and authentic. We cover this in more detail in Chapter 8, "Brand Stewardship."

Understanding the generational differences within an organization can go a long way toward building an open organization. At the risk of oversimplifying, there are three major groups we observed during our discussions with Tasti D-Lite home office associates. The correlation to baby boomers, generation Xers, and millennials should be clear, but we came up with different names.

In the oldest group we found that safety and privacy were at a premium when it came to the Internet. This *freedom genera-tion* sees the value of personal connections and relationships but may feel as if their liberty is at risk when they go online. For many people in this demographic, their freedom is sacrosanct. Supply chain manager Gary Foltynewicz's perspective on his generation is interesting, "We feel we are losing part of our-selves every time we go online and our personal data are being collected."

The folks in the middle are a little more comfortable with sharing, but they are quite selective and pragmatic in that there needs to be a value exchange. There has to be a purpose to the interaction. We call them the *value generation*. Operations coordinator Tamela Gibson offers, "If a business doesn't have a website, I'm probably not going to go there because I don't know what to expect. I want to see if it has specials, and what new things are going on. We're looking for value." When it comes to who is behind a brand, she adds, "I'd rather see a coupon than a CEO. Unless of course the CEO is holding a coupon."

We label the younger group the *digital generation*. Here the web is seen as a source of information and entertainment. People of this generation are quite comfortable with sharing, and they are more likely to identify themselves with a brand online than those of other generations. Representing this group for us is marketing coordinator Jade Fox who is on the front line listening and interacting with customers at the corporate level. "As a member of our demographic, it's easy for me to commu-nicate with, and respond to, people who are like me. The fact that I am also a health conscious individual allows me the ability to relate to our customers even more." She adds, "People have come to expect that we are listening constantly and will respond to their comments quickly. Customers appreciate this connec-tion because it fits better with their busy lifestyles. You do not have to call a 1-800 number between 9 a.m. and 5 p.m., while you're conveniently at work, and wait on the line for an hour to get an answer. There's no longer a wall standing between you and the brand you love."

It's easy to see how the comfort level of each group changes over time, but everyone has something to bring to the table when it comes to a corporate approach to transparency. Understanding the differences in each group will go far toward creating a culture in which members of all groups can feel as though they can contribute something that is valued.

Regardless of age, everyone can listen. People may have different reactions to what they see when it comes to the content that is created online, but most will recognize the value that it can bring to the business. The responses can range from "Why would someone share that?" to "Oh, this is going on Facebook!" We suspect that you've heard these kinds of remarks in your organization.

Old Dogs, New Tricks?

We asked some seasoned professionals the question, "What is more challenging, teaching a young, digital native good business acumen, or teaching an older person online social skills?" Social-savvy grandmother Deb Evans says,

> When it comes to the older generation, they have to be taught online skills like blogging, how to use Twitter, Facebook, or LinkedIn for business. To digital natives, these technologies are intuitive. Even my grandson understands things like swipe versus type because it's more natural. What doesn't come natural to them is how to deal with a business crisis or issues with customers because they just don't have the experience. The mature workforce is now starting to understand the need for social media, but they're not quite sure how to use it. I think the success will be when you've got your seasoned executives managing and monitoring what's going on with social media, but they may not be the hands-on, day-to-day person. They've got to work very closely with the younger members of the workforce in

executing the social media strategy. It has to be team-
work. It has to be leaders working with their teams,
guiding, directing, and facilitating what needs to be said
in social media, where the digital natives will know how
to execute it, but they may not understand the message
itself. That's where the leadership has to pick a role and
be present.

Gary Foltynewicz develops innovative logistics solutions for
both Tasti D-Lite and Planet Smoothie. Without disclosing his
age, we'll just say that he's been keeping retirement at bay for
some time. Gary says,

> The younger generation will need to understand the
> application of business principles as well as learn verbal
> communication and relationship management skills. It
> seems that the more we get involved in the digital age,
> the greater potential we have to lose the personal touch
> that we had 20 or 30 years ago. Teaching these interper-
> sonal skills to the younger generation seems equally as
> hard as teaching the technical skills to the older genera-
> tion. I think for the latter there may need to be some
> financial incentives.

Social Feedback

One of the fundamental shifts in mindset that the digital generation brings is the real-time feedback response of peers. The
ability to like, +1, retweet, and promote or demote a social status
update is providing us with immediate responses to our actions
or opinions. This concept is bleeding over into workplace
performance.

John Havens is executive vice president of strategy and
engagement for Yoxi (Yoxi.tv), an organization that discovers
and highlights social entrepreneurs. He speaks and writes about
emerging media and is coauthor of *Tactical Transparency: How*

Leaders Can Leverage Social Media to Maximize Value and Build Their Brand (Jossey-Bass, 2008). We talked with John about his ideas and how the transparent workplace has started to incorporate these elements. "Millennials and younger people are much more used to this mindset of the transparent workplace. Why shouldn't your manager be able to aggregate feedback in real time about your work? A social-friendly workforce could easily provide an environment where performance can be measured faster and more accurately."

In fact, platforms like Rypple (acquired by Salesforce late in 2011) are being used within organizations to do just that. Imagine project management software meets social network meets collaboration application. This internal Facebook-like methodology is making waves in the HR world as departments are moving away from annual self-evaluations to real-time community-based evaluations. Staying competitive in the transparent workplace means receiving and incorporating feedback at a much faster rate.

John continues, "It's not just about your being transparent anymore. If someone at work is a jerk and is really hurting the company, I could give a thumbs down to his actions and provide actionable specifics. If others could submit comments on those actions as well and if the manager is able to click on a button and understand the issues in real time versus months down the road, this is going to start to have major seismic shifts within a company."

John explains that companies not willing to consider these kinds of technologies don't understand the mindset of those now entering the workforce. "It's not just that they're archaic for not embracing these tools and digital methodologies, they just don't understand the younger generation. It's in their DNA to have this feedback loop. However, the focus is not primarily about the tools. The tools are simply a reflection of the mindset."

Now imagine extending that mindset beyond the individuals within the office and capturing the bigger picture. The possibilities to drive efficiencies in things like project management, supply chain distribution, and vendor relationships are staggering. Having a feedback loop with a shorter cycle time has the potential to impact just about any kind of business.

Beyond Big Brother

The top-down big brother mentality is being replaced by peer review and real-time feedback. John Havens says, "If people are truly passionate about their work and they are there because they really want to be, then this is not judgmental accountability. Any peer or self-critique would be constructive and supportive of passionate commitment toward the ideals of an organization. Knowing that I can be observed so I can improve professionally and bring value to the company should be important to me."

Won't employees feel threatened by this kind of microscopic attention and scrutiny? Or will this simply provide a better way to increase job satisfaction and quickly get to the heart of why people are there?

Companies have spent millions over the past decade on monitoring and productivity software to track employee activity like Internet abuse and application usage. Protecting computer systems and measuring the effectiveness of associates is obviously still vital, but what would happen if companies spent as much time and energy finding out what customers are saying and doing on the web?

In the future there will be two types of companies: those that monitor and stifle the social activity of their employees and those that empower the social activity of their employees. In our case, the latter is extended to franchisees. There is no doubt that in many organizations the fundamental shift in mindset will be profound.

A Personal Journey (as Told by BJ)

Like many other companies, our initial venture into the depths of social media came partly as a response and desire to impact search engine rankings. Having a background that included web development and organic search engine optimization (SEO), I was closest to the topic, given the size of Tasti D-Lite at the time. As it turned out, my other related experience with business intelligence (BI) and customer relationship management (CRM) was just as important. In all other regards I was the typical director of information technology type. Development of enterprise level systems for franchise organizations filled most of my time and my résumé for the previous dozen years. Technology has always been my second language, and the running joke is that I was once president of my high school audio-visual club. (I have pictures.)

Emerging from the server closet one afternoon early in 2008, I was approached by Jim and Peter to discuss a new endeavor. We had just recently started to put our social negligence behind us with a new and more interactive website, but it was time to look beyond that presence and start participating in other ways of sharing the Tasti D-Lite story online. If the brand had thrived for over 20 years by word of mouth, extending that conversation into the virtual realm had real potential. "Mashing up" that content would, hypothetically, start influencing search engine rankings. Understanding something called social media optimization became the first task.

We started with a blog and then jumped into Facebook's new business pages and something altogether different called Twitter. Unaware of what would come next, I fell headlong into this new frontier and haven't taken the time to look back since. As a result, my IT DNA has been permanently corrupted for the better. The more I listened to the activity around our brand, the more it permeated my mindset, and part of my responsibility became imparting those valuable insights to others within the organization and ultimately to integrate them into our enterprise.

There are some things I would have done differently from the start. For whatever reason, I waited a full year after managing the main @tastidlite Twitter account to create my individual account @bj_emerson. Had I known that managing a personal brand was in the cards, that year could have been helpful in establishing more connections. In the same way, I signed up only for Facebook initially to create the brand page. I mean, why would an IT guy need these things except to create the corporate accounts? Who would expect appearances on CBNC, numerous publications including the *New York Times, Financial Times, Inc. Magazine,* dozens of speaking engagements, mentions in seven different books, five different industry awards, and of all things attendance at a Hollywood movie premier? When I saw that the University of Iowa and others were including our social media efforts within their curriculum and exams, I thought for sure that the ride had to end soon, but it hasn't. In addition, the momentum online has not waned. The more we invest in rewarding our loyal customers and finding innovative ways to enhance the customer experience, the more our efforts just keep giving back.

Figuring out how to use these new social tools to give customers back the hugs they'd been giving us has been a highlight of my career. When I speak to marketing audiences, I encourage them to venture into the IT department and find someone who can help them with social technologies. Conversely, when I'm talking to IT audiences, I'll invite them to go back to their corporate office and start empowering the marketing and communications folks with these new tools. I've been privileged to be able to tell our story.

To be fair, some IT people belong in the server closet. They are happy there. But as you read this book, I hope you'll discover that just about anyone has the ability to create and curate great content, cultivate stronger relationships, and be a storyteller.

As it turns out, IT people can be human.

Social IT People?

A social IT person is an oxymoron in many organizations, but IT people can hold some inherent and often hidden advantages. Here are several reasons for getting them involved in the race for transparency:

1. From a listening perspective, they are naturals at monitoring things. If they are good at watching over the online habits of employees, think about how good they could be at keeping an eye on customers.
2. They understand security and privacy. Venturing into the social realm will be a hurdle for some at first, but having this mindset as a foundation can help keep an organization out of trouble.
3. They know how to measure stuff. Understanding the points of measurement and how to capture key data points in online campaigns is critical for determining return on investment. Those responsible for gathering vital intelligence in other areas of the business can bring a perspective and skillset that others may not have.
4. They know how to automate and integrate systems and applications. With so many different networks and platforms, you'll need help understanding what is possible when you're trying to get processes and information flowing.
5. They have no marketing box they need to think outside of. This could be argued both ways, but on today's web, this is not a bad thing.
6. They have a shorter learning curve when it comes to learning new technologies.
7. At the end of the day, if you can't trust the IT people, then you have bigger problems than lack of transparency.

We asked Jason Yusko, director of information systems for the International Franchise Association, why the IT department should be included in social efforts. He said, "Whenever you are looking at the new applications of social media, you need to be taking into account how they can integrate with legacy systems. There needs to be someone in the organization with a base understanding and knowledge of the technologies behind it."

There are certainly arguments that can be made for including any discipline in online efforts. Just like our generational examples above, each will have their own strengths to bring to the table. Disciplines like communications, marketing, and PR will naturally have much to bring in the shift toward openness. Depending on the size of the organization, these initiatives can literally be born out of any department. Legal is another department that is critical when it comes to social media. See Chapter 11, "The Social Future," for some insights on the legal department of the future.

The Heart of the Matter

The Velveteen Rabbit wanted to be real, but he was concerned about the pain that might be involved. "It doesn't happen all at once," said the Skin Horse. "You become. It takes a long time. That's why it doesn't happen to people who break easily, or have sharp edges, or who have to be carefully kept."

Indeed, rubbing up against others in life can be abrasive. We hope that by this time, you see the value in it.

The more transparent you are for yourself and for others, the more likely you are to want to give something of value while you are receiving something of value. This makes for a better deal at every level. From the private equity and acquisition merger level all the way down to people who are consuming products from businesses at the line level.

You have to assume that the implication and result will be positive. If you don't, what it means is that you will lose customers, revenue, and profit. If you aren't more consumer-friendly, you are going to lose business faster and be less successful. The transparency has to reveal something of value and be beneficial to you and your customer.

The foundation for a transparent life is openness, respect, and accountability. If you are not touching people, you have no relationship. Scaling issues aside, if the mechanism is not understood, if it is not real, it doesn't work. Over time, it has to be real.

In *Delivering Happiness: A Path to Profits, Passion, and Purpose* (Business Plus, 2010), Tony Hsieh, the CEO of Zappos, writes,

"For individuals, character is destiny. For organizations, culture is destiny." So culture is to corporations as character is to individuals.

From here we explore what it means to have character within one of these social channels—Twitter.

CHAPTER 4

Character in 140 Characters

When words are many, sin is not absent,
but he who holds his tongue is wise.
—Proverbs 10:19

D escribed as the SMS (Short Message Service) of the Internet, Twitter enables users to share 140 character updates, links, and pictures with anyone who cares to follow along. While people may be sharing less within each post or update, ultimately more information is being created, most of which is public.

For businesses, this very personal and often protective community requires engagement that is not only authentic but timely as well. Here conversations typically start and end within minutes. Responding in only 140 characters at a time can require a creative touch because the spirit of the response can be just as important as what is said.

The Twitter community is generally responsive to an authentic approach, and most members of that community will honor and defend people who demonstrate fairness and sincerity. Consistently packaging just the right personality and character within a limited space is challenging but can be extremely rewarding. Placing this critical voice on the front lines of a brand requires finding and keeping the right talent.

An open social network is an awesome thing. It allows both the best and worst of humanity and life to be on display for all who care to observe. The raw, unfiltered passion, emotion, and interaction can be fascinating. Like-minded people who share values or interests generally gravitate toward one another for support and information.

The follower model on Twitter makes for an interesting popularity gala where your level of acceptance and your following are largely determined by the value you provide. This value is usually in the form of relevant and credible information, interaction, or at least some level of entertainment.

There are, of course, those who are already so well-known through other media that millions are certain to follow even if they suspect it is not actually the individual doing the posting. Many use so-called ghost writers to help populate their Twitter feed. Celebrities and politicians aside, earning a true organic following on Twitter does not come easily. The reception that awaits businesses looking to get in on the action can vary widely. As you would expect, the sheer scale of larger brands with a global footprint (and marketing budget) will obviously draw the masses. The amount of user interaction for these businesses keeps entire teams of PR, marketing, and customer service reps at the ready.

The timing surrounding Tasti D-Lite's entry into the social realm coincided with the expansion of some exciting platforms. MySpace seemed to have run its course, brands were just getting started on Facebook which was emerging hot and heavy, and Twitter was at its genesis. The opportunities at this time were unique. While there wasn't an enormous amount of dialogue taking place, we saw enough to know that there was great value in being a part of the conversations that were there. The real-time and public nature of Twitter has provided a steady stream of unfiltered comments and continues to be an endless source of great feedback and insights for Tasti D-Lite and Planet Smoothie.

Brittany Weiner
@ilovenycfood

"sometimes you want to go where everybody knows your name"…for me, that is @tastidlite

Everybody knows: Brittany shares her thoughts publicly on Twitter.

To Follow or Not to Follow

Many people will follow businesses on Twitter simply to get deals, coupons, and promotions as if to say that this is the only value they expect from a faceless brand icon. They will disengage just as quickly if the feed does not continue to merit their attention. It would make sense that value tolerance and expectations are higher for brand accounts than for those of personal profiles. We are representing the commercial interests of a business that provides a service or product after all. Spewing out pointless updates to clutter the Twittersphere is a great way to get ignored.

As we covered in Chapter 3, "Going Behind the Brand," we all look for reasons to disqualify businesses and marketers both online and off. More information gives us more opportunities to eliminate brand A or brand B. Any sign of inconsistent behavior or a discrepancy in character gives us an out. As a result, selecting a vendor, merchant, or brand online has never been easier. The unfollow button is a powerful thing.

It should go without saying at this point that Twitter has become a critical communication and listening tool for businesses large and small.

Emotional Labor

All this human interaction and communication require energy, but is using social media any different from what a call center representative might do or what would typically be handled through another customer service channel? Consider the various elements at play here. On any given day on Twitter one can find opportunities in the following categories:

1. Customer service support
2. Lead generation and sales
3. Brand messaging
4. Reputation management/PR
5. Competitor analysis
6. Crisis management

Depending on the nature of the conversation, there's a wide range of emotional energy and creativity required. Aside from the great amounts of information that need to be available, the 24/7 real-time activity and opportunity will require some discretionary energy to go beyond the norm and deliver a great experience. We talk about resource management in Chapter 6, "You Can't Outsource Relationships."

You Must Be Present to Win

We believe that Twitter is here to stay, but we also realize that it is just one example of how consumers are using social networking to interact. History has shown that these communities rise and fall in popularity and that users are likely to migrate to other sites over time. What this means for businesses is that wherever there is discussion about a product or service, there is not only opportunity but ultimately a responsibility to be part of the dialogue.

Unless you're a megabrand, a celebrity, or some other icon, doing nothing other than pushing out periodic updates won't get you far on any social network. As we'll see, being present means listening, responding to the good as well as the bad, and proactively engaging and pursuing customers from time to time.

Listening Versus Hearing

There are significant differences in the approaches that can be used when you monitor the conversations of customers. A strategy that involves merely tracking conversations for the purpose of reputation management falls short if there is no intention of actually caring about what else customers might be saying. This important point deserves a refresher on how hearing and listening are two very different activities.

Hearing is simply the passive, involuntary reception of sound. We can hear indifferently. We have the ability to hear because it is necessary for protection and survival. Listening, on the other hand, is optional. The intentional act of focused listening with the goal of understanding requires energy. Beyond general awareness, listening is a process of evaluation and a determined focus on others at a particular level of detail.

In short, listening is about understanding. While hearing involves just a set of ears and a minimal amount of cognitive function, listening requires discipline and true selflessness. When applied to marketing, brand management, and customer relations, you'll see a great contrast—one that customers can also see and feel. Emotional connections and real relationships can be built only on this kind of listening.

Unfortunately, this important skill is one of the least developed in the C-suite. Culturally, the listening posture needs to come from the top down in an organization. Done effectively, the impact on the bottom line would be immediate through the increased quality of both internal and external relationships. Generally people, and customers, will say what they are thinking if someone is listening. Everybody wants to be heard, and many times you don't even have to ask the question.

Listening is a message in and of itself. If customers know that a business is actively and consistently listening on a social network like Twitter, they are more likely to make mention of their use of or experience with a product or service. While these experiences can be positive or negative, the value to a business should be clear.

Who Has Time for All This?

The sheer volume of information on Twitter can be overwhelming. The signal-to-noise ratio can be quite low unless you know what to look for and how to find it. There are many tools to help automate functions to find valuable information and connections, but we really need to start at a change in mindset in order to address this concern.

In Chapter 3, "Going Behind the Brand," we discuss the value of transparency. Understanding the potential that the networks can have for individuals as well as businesses is just the start. Sites like Twitter and LinkedIn can be easily more effective than traditional networking, which certainly takes a great amount of time and energy. Start replacing those activities with learning new tools so that you can connect with others.

Tackling one social network at a time may be the best approach for those who feel overwhelmed by social media. Because of the real-time nature of Twitter, public searches can easily return a wealth of information on a regular basis.

What Do Consumers Expect?

With new social channels opening up online, customer grievances are being aired freely on the networks where consumers interact. Are customers really expecting businesses to respond when they tweet complaints? A September 2011 Maritz Research study revealed that the expectation for interaction has risen as more brands are coming online. It is also interesting to note that older users have higher expectations than younger users.

With respect to reputation management, it would make sense that brands responding on Twitter are viewed more positively than those that do not. Also according to the Maritz study, nearly 75 percent of the users were either very satisfied or somewhat satisfied with the response they received to a complaint. This would seem to indicate that using Twitter as a customer service channel is quite effective.[1]

It would also seem logical that as more brands start to answer the social phone so-to-speak, the tolerance for that social negligence we speak of earlier would decrease over time.

Lost in Translation

Being relevant online means not only understanding individual statements but understanding the context of the statements as well. For Twitter (and in life), real listening takes time to understand the context of the conversation. Drive-by, out-of-context participation will not only annoy people, but it will also damage credibility. Integrity means capturing the full story and picture from the perspective of the user.

In the same way, being clueless in the conversation does not generally turn out well. While unfiltered customer comments never cease to surprise and inspire us, the creativity and passion found in the online discussion can require a little translation from time to time. Here we use a Planet Smoothie example:

 Taelor

This Planet Smoothie is too clutch right now

Too clutch?: Translation, please.

Depending on your age, you may need to have the Urban Dictionary at the ready. In this particular case the sentiment is positive with *clutch* meaning great, essential, and potent.

Loyalty

Finding and connecting with brand advocates has never been easier. People talk (and tweet) about the products and services they love. While that can certainly go the other way, creating virtual touch points on Twitter with those having an affinity for a brand is a big part of social CRM which we introduce in Chapter 2, "The Race for Transparency." Taking advantage of the opportunity to keep conversations going and develop long-term connections with these advocates is critical for businesses wanting to create community within the general Twitter population.

 @vanillabean45
Karen Nicole Costa

Oh boy. This Pinkberry experience blows. This is getting a yelp review... I shall never cheat on you again @tastidlite you forever have my <3

Cheater?: Karen comes clean and reveals her allegiance.

Don't Be Boring

Over time, we've seen both good and bad examples of companies finding and communicating their voice online. While some jump in with both feet and experiment as they go along, others develop extensive strategies around content and voice. Customers can usually tell the difference and have been known to provoke companies just to see what kind of response they will receive, if any. They are pleasantly surprised from time to time if the reply is not as expected, especially when there is a personal touch and they feel they have the attention of a real human being.

An entire industry is forming around content marketing for social channels. The ongoing challenge for online marketers will be creating higher-quality and more engaging material that will stand out and rise above the noise.

 **@tastidlite**
Tasti D-Lite

Ice Cream Flavor Name Generator: quizopolis.com/icecream-name-... What's your flavor name?

Don't be boring: Creative content starts conversations.

Fortunately, customers can be great sources of stories and material that can be "retweeted" or shared with the rest of the community.

 **@tastidlite**
Tasti D-Lite

Yikes. Look out! ;) RT @SelenaCoppock: If I don't have some Tasti D Lite soon, I will fistfight someone. #addictedtoTastiDLite

Fistfight!: Customers are great sources of creative content.

Lurking and Flocking

Social media and Twitter in particular have introduced many new terms to our vocabulary. Some definitions are in order along with an explanation of what each might have to do with loyalty and brand building.

Lurking

According to Wikipedia, the vast majority of users within online groups are lurkers who read discussions but rarely or never participate actively. The Urban Dictionary offers this simple definition: "A lurker is someone that follows the forum but doesn't post." According to an early study on lurkers, a lack of trust is one of the reasons for this behavior.[2] We touch on this issue in Chapter 11, "The Social Future."

In any social network, the challenge becomes turning these lurkers into engaged followers. This starts with knowing they exist and are at least involved on some level. Any given campaign or post can result in a response from someone who has been silent for months or longer. While you never know who is listening in, the fun really starts when you can get them talking.

Flocking

In a keynote address to the Direct Marketing Association in 2011 cofounder and creative director of Twitter, Biz Stone, said, "The mechanization of 'flocking' is rudimentary with birds and fish, with the behavior of one influencing all the others. We had never seen that before with humans, but it's what is so incredibly powerful about Twitter."

There are many examples of users on Twitter rallying around a cause or campaign. The unique way information travels on this platform makes it easy to discover what topics and issues are popular and currently trending.

When the conversation is public, don't be afraid to introduce yourself to others; be prepared to extend a hand, offer an insight, or demonstrate some value. The etiquette is no different from that of a physical networking event, just more open. You're more likely to be received well when you ask for nothing in return but simply add to the discussion. Hijacking a conversation by injecting something out of context is not going to be received well, so don't change the subject in a self-serving way.

Becoming a part of most trending conversations on Twitter will require an understanding of hashtags.

The Almighty Hashtag (#)

Popular conversations can not only spread very rapidly, but they can remain escalated for days. Trending topics that identify the most popular current conversations are usually marked with a pound sign or "hashtag" such as #JustinBieber. Conversations are tied together by these powerful yet simple marks so users can easily search and find all associated comments. When a topic is started or grows viral, the hashtag ties possibly thousands of posts together so more users can become aware of the issue. The topic could be breaking news, current events, or just good jokes. Trending topics are usually not a joke for brands, however. They could be the best thing to happen to a brand, or they could spell disaster for a brand's PR.

One of the great benefits of using hashtags is the value that can be derived from the backchannel of conversation during events, conferences, or even television shows. A simple search on Twitter allows users to connect conversations through a common keyword preceded by a pound (#) sign. This yields all the related content created by those who have included the hashtag within their tweet. Used in this way at a live event, an interesting dynamic unfolds that enhances the conversation and interaction. It can be just as valuable and insightful as the event content itself. Many times hashtags can provide a glimpse into the mind of the audience and reveal things that might otherwise go unsaid.

Go to just about any conference, concert, or large event these days and take a look at what is happening in the virtual realm. You'll see a fascinating dynamic taking place. People are connecting around the event in real time via mobile devices, tablets, and laptops on Twitter as well as on location-based applications.

Discussions about the event as it is happening reflect what the group is thinking. The mind of the audience is being shared in a way never before possible. This backchannel is chock full of real conversations conducted by people who are sharing the same experience. Ice-breaking exchanges here can facilitate introductions. The amount of information that can be gathered through online profiles can tell you instantly whether or not this is someone who has a common interest with you. More on the future of personal and business networking in Chapter 11, "The Social Future."

Just Try It

At the next event or conference you attend, find out if a hashtag is being used. Set up a search at http://hashtags.org or http://search.twitter.com to view the conversations by entering the hashtag. You don't need a Twitter account to listen in. If you do have an account, be sure to use the hashtag in your tweets because others will be listening as well. Some events will even have an overhead display of these tweets so people attending the event can see the conversation.

FIVE BENEFITS OF USING CONFERENCE HASHTAGS
1. Preevent chatter gets the conversation started, and others can learn about the event and follow along remotely.
2. Introductions are streamlined as attendees break the ice on Twitter before meeting in person.
3. Real-time virtual conversations during sessions allow everyone to participate when their voice and insights may not have been heard otherwise. Questions can be asked without interrupting the flow of the physical presentation.
4. Speakers and event producers can solicit and collect valuable unfiltered feedback from attendees.
5. Postevent tweets allow the conversations and connections to continue.

Don't be afraid to start your own viral hashtag. Everyday users on Twitter create new hashtags for all kinds of conversations. There are no restrictions; you are only bound by the 140-character limit and your own imagination.

@whiticisms
Whitney Young

Just spent my last $5 on Tasti D-Lite. Judge me. #epictweets

Judge me: Whitney uses the popular hashtag #epictweets.

A Tasti Tweetup

Combine the classic meetup networking event with Twitter, and you have a tweetup. Tweetups are offline meetings that can generate online buzz and offer merchants an opportunity to interact both on and offline.

The first tweetup we held in New York was an interesting experiment in community engagement. Why would anyone attend an event sponsored by a brand at a retail location? What could we possibly offer that would draw a crowd? The tweetup was not a complete disaster, but it provided some great lessons for future meetings:

1. Had we not been investing in the various online communities through regular contests and promotions well before the event, no one would have shown up. Many of the attendees were contest winners and people we regularly had engaged with on Twitter and Facebook. Our demonstrating a genuine interest in others provided a return.
2. Offering some fun around our product gave people a reason to spread the word before and during about the event. Special tweetup flavors like peanut butter hashtag and maple fudge microblog were served as well as a "Fail Whale" cake. (The Fail Whale is a graphic that is displayed

on the Twitter website when the network is overloaded and inaccessible.) The highlight was the best swirl contest where contestants pull their own Tasti from our soft-serve machines after a quick training session. Once presented to a panel of judges, votes are cast, and a winner is awarded with a TreatCard or other prize. Capturing these moments to share online can make for some great blog posts and YouTube content.

3. Exclusive offers on Tasti products for attendees are promoted as part of the event. Sampling new products allows guests to try the latest line extensions.

Fail Whale: We created this Fail Whale cake at one of our early tweetups in New York City.

Hosting an offline meeting for those that are active online can be a great introduction to local groups or organizations. During the event the conversation will no doubt spread within the social networks. Area social media clubs often look for venues to hold meetings and make presentations, usually involving technology and social media. Many of the members are marketers and solutions providers. Sponsoring an event for these leaders and influencers is another way to effectively connect with members and establish credibility online as well as off. There's no brick-and-mortar presence required to contribute to these kinds of events, and they can do wonders for an online presence for just about any business.

Tasti Trivia

A fundamental difference between Twitter and other social networks is the instant messaging atmosphere that exists which can make for some interesting contests and interactive campaigns. While desktop software can be used, the inherent mobility of the application allows users to participate from just about anywhere at any time with their mobile devices.

Holding a live trivia contest requires some preparation and forethought in order for it to be executed effectively. Done correctly, both the host and the contestants are in for a fun but frantic interchange.

 Tasti D-Lite
@tastidlite

Q4: What is the current @foursquare Mayor special at Tasti D-Lite Times Square NYC? #TastiTrivia – Include the hashtag in your answer!

 Scott Markman
@ScottMarkman

@tastidlite 1 FREE SMALL CUP OR CONE PER WEEK #TastiTrivia

 Tasti D-Lite
@tastidlite

A4: The answer is: 1 Free Small Cup or Cone per Week. Congrats to our winner @scottMarkman DM your email address please. #TastiTrivia

Tasti trivia: This sample exchange with Scott shows how the trivia Q&A works.

Below are some tips to help you pull off a successful trivia contest. (Disclaimer: Be sure to check Twitter's current policies for running contests and promotions.)

1. If you do not have a regularly set time for periodic contests, give the community advance notice of at least one hour, and promote the contest several times within that hour.
2. Avoid using the term "contest" in your tweets. This is a commonly searched word that may draw the attention of some who simply troll the Internet to win prizes.
3. Use a hashtag to tie the posts together. Be sure to communicate what the hashtag is from the beginning, and use it within every question, answer, and supporting post.
4. Establish some ground rules just before the start time such as:
   a. Only the first answer per Twitter account will count. This will keep people from guessing and force them to do some research.
   b. Answers will not count unless they include the proper hashtag.
   c. Only one win per Twitter account per contest session will be allowed.
5. As an optional bonus, let participants know that two winners will be selected at random from among all who provide an answer to all the trivia questions.
6. Prepare every tweet ahead of time in a document so there will be as little typing as possible. For each question there should be four posts:
   a. Let participants know what the prize is for the first correct answer.
   b. Ask the question.
   c. Provide the correct answer and announce who the winner is.
   d. Let them know when the next question is coming. Keep this time frame short to keep their attention.

7. Don't make the questions easy. You'll be surprised at how resourceful Twitter users are. They may have others helping them.
8. You'll need to monitor the tweets in a hashtag utility that automatically refreshes every few seconds. It will be important to know the exact order of the answers in case there is a debate.

 @jennimacdonald
Jennifer MacDonald

I'm gonna win a Tasti coffee mug someday! RT @tastidlite: Wow, that was a crazy #TastiTrivia session! Congrats to our 7 winners.

Someday!: Jenni shares her thoughts after a Tasti trivia session.

Providing rapid-fire engagement for followers will strengthen the relationship and keep them on their toes for future promotions. Aside from others seeing these conversations and joining the fun, this is one way to maintain and reinforce a high signal-to-noise ratio within a Twitter feed. Forming this impression in followers is critical for strengthening top-of-mind awareness.

Exploring the Boundaries

There's a fine line between creepy and creative customer engagement. Just where that line falls is different for any given brand. Understanding how much customers will tolerate or embrace is going to require a great amount of experience with and knowledge of those customers.

Manager of design and construction Alex Bernard offered this: "Some companies go overboard on how much they share. You want to stay top of mind. You want them to stay engaged, but if you go too far with it, it just gets weird."

On April 1 one year we posted the following on our main Twitter account:

Tasti D-Lite
@tastidlite

VIDEO: Man caught hiding Tasti D-Lite under his
trenchcoat: http:/bit.ly/82cBh

Trenchcoat Tasti: Be on the lookout for practical jokes on April 1.

The link sent followers to the 1980s Rick Astley video *Never Gonna Give You Up* on YouTube. This popular Internet meme and bait-and-switch practical joke is known as "RickRolling." The elements of RickRolling usually include a prankster who sends a disguised hyperlink to an unsuspecting victim in the hopes that the victim clicks through to the disruptive video. Fall prey to this in an office with your speakers turned on and everyone knows you've been RickRolled. That's just good fun. The challenge then becomes figuring out ways to get others to click through to the video at awkward and inappropriate times.

The only follower bold enough to reply was Lisa:

@crazykarafan
Lisa

@tastidlite Damn, I've been RickRolled!

RickRolled!: Lisa confesses to being a victim of our practical joke.

What did we expect would happen from this kind of interaction? Does it really matter? Throwing the proverbial mud on the wall to see what will stick is a big part of finding your way within these online communities. Trying to stay spontaneous while attempting to measure any results can be tricky.

So what were the results? Unfortunately, the shortened URL that we used in this example was shared with many others who were playing the same trick on that April Fools' Day. We could access the analytics provided by the URL shortener that was used, but we could not accurately track the number of clicks that would tell us how many followers actually took the bait. From an engagement standpoint, some of our followers who found themselves watching the video may not have understood the joke and may have been really confused. For those who did understand it, feedback may have been withheld because they did not want to admit they got fooled.

Character within these communities means being creative. We talk more about how to avoid being boring in Chapter 5, "Don't Be Boring (and Other Thoughts on Relevance)."

Tasti Found Me

Connections on Twitter can be established in a number of ways. Some people may stumble across conversations others are having with a business. Others go out and actively look for brands with which they want to identify. One of Twitter's unique differences is the ability for businesses to proactively connect.

Our survey question posed to Twitter followers, "How did you find Tasti D-Lite on Twitter?" yielded some interesting results:

Just searched for it and found it on Twitter	32.7%
Tasti found me and followed me first	25.4%
Saw others having conversation with @tastidlite on Twitter and followed	14.5%
Heard or read about Tasti's Twitter efforts offline	9.1%
A friend was following Tasti on Twitter	9.1%
Saw it on the Tasti website	5.4%
Other	0.8%

Specific responses included:

"Tasti started following me after I tweeted about an afternoon snack."

"Tasti started following me. I figured I'd return the favor."

"You started following me first."

"They found me and responded to me when I checked in on 4 square."

Fun with Celebrities

An objective look at the profile of Tasti D-Lite would uncover a celebrity appeal that has been enjoyed by the brand for many years. Along with the cult following of regular customers, these associations have helped to elevate the brand to new heights and have helped validate the brand identity. Photos of popular personalities enjoying their frozen treats have been collected from various sources and include Heidi Klum, Taylor Swift, Emmy Rossum, George Stephanopoulos, Paul Rudd, and Téa Leoni among many others.

How to Engage a Celeb

Much better than mere sightings, we love it when we have the opportunity to have direct conversations with celebrities about their Tasti experience. Take for example the day we found actress/singer Emmy Rossum sharing her experience with her 48,000 followers. Known for her roles in the films *Phantom of the Opera* and *The Day After Tomorrow* as well as numerous TV shows, she apparently has a thing for Italian food and Tasti D-Lite and has no qualms about sharing it with anyone who cares to listen.

Emmy Rossum
@emmyrossum

Walking down the street wit the wind in my face carrying take-out Italian food & tasti-d-lite 2/multiple topping options = happiness

Happiness: Emmy Rossum shares an update with followers.

So what do you do when you see this kind of conversation? The marketer in each of us would want to keep the conversation going. The PR person in each of us would want to tell everyone else that Emmy Rossum loves Tasti D-Lite. The risk management officer in each of us might advise her against texting while walking. So what would the human being within each of us do?

A carefully worded question can sometimes keep the conversation going, which allows more people to learn about Tasti D-Lite. Our response:

 Tasti D-Lite @tastidlite

Hey @emmyrossum glad you enjoyed it, but you didn't say what flavor. Got a favorite?

Tell us more: A carefully posed question can keep them talking.

 Emmy Rossum @emmyrossum

Rockin' out w smores & rainbow sprinkles now! RT @ tastidlite Hey @emmyrossum glad u enjoyed it, but u didn't way what flavor. Got a favorite?

Rockin': Emmy shares her response with everyone.

The key thing to note here is how she fashioned her response. For those not familiar with the vernacular, her reply was appended to our question. This effectively forwarded it to all of her followers and made our Twitter handle visible so that others could easily follow @tastidlite. This type of promotion can go both ways as you can see from our response.

 Tasti D-Lite @tastidlite

RT @emmyrossum: Rockin' out w smores & rainbow sprinkles now! – Woo hoo!

Woo hoo!: Our final exchange shared Emmy's response with our followers.

In another example, MTV reality star Whitney Port had the following to share with her 393,595 followers:

whitneyEVEport
whitney port

i could not be more excited.... a tasti d lite just opened around the corner from my apartment!

Tasti D-Lite
@tastidlite

@whitneyEVEport Got a favorite flavor we can put on tap? ;)

whitneyEVEport
whitney port

Mint chocolate chip!?! RT @ tastidlite: @whitneyEVEport Got a favorite flavor we can put on tap? ;)

Got a favorite?: This exchange let us know what Whitney's favorite flavor was for future reference.

By this time you should see the opportunity that exists here to do something around the personality and the flavor of the local store. (More on the execution of these types of engagements in other chapters.)

When Taylor Swift tweeted about Tasti to her followers, the volume of inquiries around, "What is Tasti D-Lite?" went off the charts. A great lesson on the importance of listening and being ready to engage should be clear.

Taylorswift13
@taylorswift13

We're getting a Tasti d lite in nashvile! YES!! Moving up in the world.

Moving up: Taylor Swift shares her excitement about Tasti D-Lite coming to Nashville.

Humility Is Better Than Celebrity

Managing a brand profile with celebrity appeal requires careful thought, particularly online where the tolerance for self-centered branding is quite low and sure to be exposed in short order. Interacting with celebs is one thing, acting like one is another. Within each community there exists a unique spirit and etiquette that is well established, maintained, and defended by the members. Understanding the differences within each will require careful observation. The rules of engagement for brands may vary, but the core requirements are honesty, authenticity, and openness. These fundamental elements of humility and transparency go much farther in both the short and long term. Businesses are typically welcomed but are kept on a short leash until they establish some hard earned credibility. While celebrity status and attitude may gain some initial attention and even appear to gain a large following, the assumptions this approach stimulates will surely prove to be a detriment in the long term.

About a year into our online efforts, Twitter published its Business 101 case studies which profiled our use of mobile coupons. Once we launched our "social friendly" TastiRewards customer loyalty program, there was quite a bit of buzz being generated, and it was hard not to share this content from time to time with our followers. One follower had this to share in response to the survey question, "What do you NOT like about Tasti's Twitter feed?":

> I'm actually thinking about unfollowing Tasti, because they're constantly tweeting about how well they use foursquare and Twitter, and how well they manage their brand through social media, etc. The occasional link is fine, but if their followers are their customers, we don't want to be reminded constantly that we're following a marketing experiment, and I work in Internet marketing, too!

Ouch! These periodic surveys allow us to see where we stand with followers and to get a perspective on how a particular channel is being managed. Sometimes the responses are hard to swallow, but they are good medicine nonetheless.

The Heart of the Matter

When it comes to loyalty and brand building, character counts. The accountability factor within communities like Twitter keeps marketers on notice, changes the parameters for acceptable behavior, and raises the bar for customer engagement. Innovation in these realms requires a real intent to meet the needs of consumers on their terms.

Communication and the element of trust need to be at the heart of what we do. The days of one-way marketing, a disregard for transparency, and force-feeding consumers are over.

True listening changes people. It enables greater understanding, clarity of relationship, and a deeper faith in others. At all levels of business and life, you can't truly listen without caring. It is essential for conflict resolution and for growing intimacy with others. Plus it brings encouragement to others that speaking can't.

Say who you are and what you need. Create value, and make sure you are listening to the response to close the loop.

CHAPTER 5

Don't Be Boring (and Other Thoughts on Relevance)

> Advertising is the cost of being boring.
> —*Andy Sernovitz, author,* Word of Mouth Marketing:
> How Smart Companies Get People Talking

The entertainment factor is a reality all content creators have to deal with. Regardless of industry, businesses are standing out by providing engaging content and capturing the eyeballs and mouse clicks of valuable customers.

Economy notwithstanding, business models are being challenged as never before. When a business model no longer supports the needs of the market because it is no longer relevant to consumers, change is imminent ready or not.

Here the worst practice is to do nothing. Waiting to see and measure the negative impact may put a business so far behind that it may not be able to recover. Being in the game at least helps the business to evolve and learn. The sidelines are a dangerous place to be in this environment.

Be Relevant; It's Cheaper

You may not care if consumers think you are boring. Perhaps your industry is not very exciting, and your customers don't really expect anything that resembles humanity. Entertaining people is one thing, but being relevant to search engines is another matter and should be of great interest to any business.

An intriguing thing has happened on the web over the last dozen years. At one time, special software would allow you to analyze the position and prominence of keywords and phrases on a website in order to rank high on popular search engines of the day like AOL. Properly optimizing and fine-tuning a site in those early dial-up days could actually yield some decent results and rankings. Link-building strategies were rampant, and it was less about what real people actually said and more about being technically relevant by making sure your code was in order. After all, what other information did search engines have to go on besides links and code?

The days of trying to fool search engines into thinking your content is relevant and authentic are over. Popularity and credibility are increasingly being determined by what others are saying about you, not what you say about you. Legitimate (and human) content is favored over automated postings or content generators. In other words, it is getting harder and harder to fool the search engines as more trustworthy conversation is generated around a business, and search results are reflecting the reality that is on the web.

While having a website in order with the appropriate meta tags (HTML code used to help identify elements of a site such as keywords) and such is still important, the massive shift toward user-generated content and conversations within social networks has changed the search engine world forever. Enter the practice of social media optimization (SMO). According to Wikipedia, social media optimization or social SEO is defined as "the methodization of social media activity with the intent of attracting unique visitors to website content. SMO is one of many online methods of website optimization."[1]

This practice was developed in response to changes in search engine algorithms that favor more dynamic content. Delivering the best search results possible based on actual popularity around a given keyword or phrase is what Google is all about. Online relevance is no longer principally defined by the target but by the conversations happening online about a business.

When it comes to advertising, the more relevant the message is, the less it will cost to share it. Being boring, however, comes at a price—a price that will continue to rise over time.

Beyond organic results, online communities and their search engines have started developing advertising models around customer response. This means that advertisers are effectively being penalized for ad content that is not relevant or engaging. Other platforms allow paid search advertisers to compete on certain keywords, but ad placement is based on how relevant the target site is to the search term.

In general, participating in the spirit of the community that has been established will be less expensive, at least in terms of hard costs. As we have established, humanness on this new web leads to effectiveness. Perhaps this chapter should be titled "Be Human, It's More Effective."

As a WSI franchise owner and Internet marketing consultant, Daren Coudriet has been in the business of helping clients connect with consumers digitally using methods such as sponsored advertising, SEO, and social media since the mid-1990s. In 2008, Daren helped us replace the preacquisition Tasti D-Lite website.

According to Daren, traditional advertising as a persuasion mechanism is continuing to lose its effectiveness. Today, it's more about finding and engaging customers with quality content and creating a two-way dialogue, not pushing advertising at them. He says, "It all comes down to being relevant. Relevancy is king. At the end of the day, Google's pursuit is to provide the most relevant content for a given keyword phrase. Two basic ways Google connects a searcher with content is through ads and organically ranked content. Relevant ads tend to earn more clicks, appear in a higher position, and most important bring the advertiser greater success and ROI." Simply put, Google rewards relevancy.

Daren continues, "Google calculates a quality score for each of the keywords that you are using in your Google Adwords campaign. It uses different factors including how relevant a keyword is to the text or content within the ad. Incorporating key words into the ad will increase the quality score. Additionally, the relevance of the landing page the ad links to affects the quality score." It is feasible then that an advertiser holding the number one spot could actually be paying less than a less relevant advertiser in the number two spot.

In short, be real and authentic, and search engines will be your friend. If you're not, get ready to pay. Organic search results are still the best way to boost traffic and allow customers to find information, but search engines are starting to look for results that have humanlike characteristics. They reward those they find and penalize the cheaters and shortcut content creators.

Twitter has developed advertising solutions for businesses. One option is promoted tweets, which are messages that can target users based on their search terms. They can also appear at or near the top of targeted users' timeline when they log on or refresh their home page.

While the formula is not revealed in detail, the Twitter website makes it clear: "Just like organic tweets, relevant and interesting messages are rewarded above all else. Tweets that engage and resonate with users will appear more frequently."[2]

The cost-per-engagement pricing model is efficient in that an advertiser pays only when someone retweets, replies to, or clicks on a promoted tweet. In short, the more engaging the tweets are, the greater the potential reach.

Facebook has long offered targeted ads for businesses and offers comprehensive tools to determine the effectiveness of ads. The extensive targeting options allow businesses to get very specific with regard to ad placement. The ads manager will show how receptive users are to a given message.

Within Facebook business pages, an "EdgeRank" algorithm determines if and when posts show up in the news feed of those who have "liked" the page. Rich media like photos and videos generally rank higher. Affinity, or prior interaction with such business pages, and time are other variables. The affinity score becomes greater as users interact with the page and they are more likely to see posts in the future. Again, interesting and engaging content is being rewarded.

When it comes to advertising online, ROI follows relevance. Aside from being cheaper, being relevant will lead to greater effectiveness when you're sharing a brand message.

Relevant Innovation

Maintaining relevance in a rapidly changing technology environment can be tricky. It seems there are new devices, social tools, and business models being created daily, any of which can serve as a temporary distraction or possibly blossom into the next great thing with opportunities that no business could survive without. Determining ahead of time which ones will die and which will have legs is not necessarily a new challenge; we just have much less time to make this decision than we did in the past.

Aside from knowing where or how to innovate, executing at just the right time in order to meet the needs of customers can be critical and requires a great deal of insight, skill, and often just plain luck. As they say about the lottery, you can't win if you don't play. Staying on the sidelines is not an option most can afford.

Forcing customers into a technology mold however can backfire. Getting too far ahead puts you in the position of pushing them into behaviors for which they are not prepared. Aside from the impact on the customer, it may be years before a technology investment pays off, if it ever does.

Falling behind the innovation curve also carries a great risk in that customers will look to get their needs met elsewhere. Meeting them where they are and deploying just before the need is realized will make all the difference. Apple Computer is a good example of a company that has managed to do this consistently.

The purpose of any customer-facing technology should be to support or provide a benefit. Meeting the needs of customers through educating, connecting, and making things more convenient should contribute to greater adoption, awareness, efficiency, and ultimately profitability.

One example of this concept has to do with the format of Tasti D-lite loyalty cards. Up until 2009, many Tasti D-Lite outlets used old-fashioned punch cards as a form of loyalty program to reward customers. Not typically recognized across locations, customers were forced to manage multiple cards, and it would not be unusual to encounter someone sorting through a dozen or more cards at the cash register. As the years went by, many people somehow grew attached to this program, as it became a part of the brand culture. This was ultimately illustrated with an unsolicited mention on the NBC show *30 Rock* with Tina Fey's character frantic when her beloved punch card had been lost. As her character put it, "Has anybody seen my wallet? It's an L.L. Bean child's wallet from the 1970s. There's no money in it, but I was one hole-punch away from a free Tasti D-Lite. Damn it to hell! I hate my life!"[3]

With this context and history behind a program, moving our core customer base to a different format and system carried with it a challenge. Clearly a more efficient mechanism for rewarding loyalty systemwide was good from a business perspective but migrating to a points-based "TastiRewards" program proved to be a stretch for some. Even with the additional benefits of the card, some customers sought the comfort of their cherished punch cards and resisted the change in format to the new plastic TreatCards.

When there was an opportunity to skip the use of physical cards altogether and move to a mobile bar code application, the context and history of the program needed to be considered. We did not want to innovate beyond what our customers were prepared to adopt.

We realize that it's not every day that these kinds of insights are broadcast on prime time TV. Interacting and listening to customers however can be just as effective.

Next we move beyond technology hurdles and address those of the human kind.

Know When to Stay Out of the Way

Business formats are shifting at a faster rate than ever before. Consumers are responding and interacting in ways never considered in both the virtual and physical realms. When it comes to the delivery of a soft-serve product, the self-serve model has emerged as an attractive and popular option in many markets. The delivery method and format are simple yet fundamentally different.

When a customer has an emotional connection with a product or service, it's usually best to stay out of the way. While it sounds simple, businesses can inadvertently put any number of things including technology and even people between customers and the object of their affection. In this case, three's a crowd. Every program, policy, or process should support and encourage this bond. So how do you make it about the customer and the product without getting in the middle?

The self-serve option now being offered in many Tasti D-Lite locations brings a new dynamic to the experience by allowing customers unfettered access to their Tasti. While full service is still available in many of these new stores, the do-it-yourself option could not get much simpler. Grab a cup, select a flavor, pull a handle.

Here an associate is available to come alongside the line of customers to provide samples and answer questions if necessary. Associates are there solely to streamline the delivery process, not to distract, slow down, or take away from it. This helps to alleviate any potential pressure a new customer might feel when expected to quickly decipher a menu and then make product, size, flavor, and topping decisions all at once.

For those who want to explore more options or see the entire menu, we can accommodate them. From no service to full service, we're prepared to cater to the full range of customer needs.

Customers want better service, but if it is just getting in the way, then it will take away from the experience. Do we really understand the value that we provide to our different customer types? How do we show our appreciation of that value? Being relevant means understanding and acting on the answers to these questions.

Finding the Sweet Spot

Here are some pointers for finding out what customers need and how they will respond to what you provide:

1. **Manage expectations.** For us, letting punch card customers know that the cards will be phased out over time helps to prepare them for what is coming up in the future. Moving toward new technologies may require some preparation in the minds of customers.

2. **Know your customers.** Insights can come only from direct interaction with those who will potentially benefit from the use of the technology. Integrate their voice in technology and product innovations. For example, do you know if it would be better to hold a best video contest or a best photo contest? These kinds of details are important when it comes to knowing what kinds of campaigns will be successful.

3. **Know the trends and be invested.** History speaks volumes when it comes to trends in customer behavior. Being personally invested in the various technology fields that affect your business will help you know where to invest.

4. **Take the time to become your customer.** This is different from listening and engaging. This has more to do with function, logistics, and implementation. Experience what your customers will experience. Put yourself in the position of using the technologies that you are asking them to adopt.

5. **Comfort levels vary, so provide options.** Forcing transparency or invading privacy can have devastating results.

Proactive or Reactive?

We've addressed the importance of listening and responding to the online activity of customers, but the reactive and defensive postures are only part of managing this presence. What if there is no activity? Sitting around waiting for customers to interact can be as much fun as watching paint dry.

So how do you know when or how to go on the offensive? For us, months of monitoring and listening gave us the confidence to actively participate in the spirit of the communities we were joining. This required a full understanding of the protocols and lingo for each. Once customers saw that we were actively sharing as well as supporting customers, the activity and conversation quickly ramped up.

Staying on the Edge

Any business managing an online presence will want to protect its investment. As the value of that presence grows, the tendency will be to become more conservative over time. We do daring things in the beginning, but it's easy to become boring over time.

Jenny Dervin of JetBlue Airways told us, "In the early days we did a lot more risk taking. The larger your audience becomes, the greater the tendency there is to play it safe, but we need to resist that." Intentionally keeping that raw edge becomes the challenge. That kind of nerve can only be fueled by the culture that supports the customers who share the voice of the brand online.

Corporate culture is important at JetBlue. Jenny offers, "You can't let anything get corporatized. We don't want to create responsibility silos as a result of anyone saying, 'That's not my job.' We pay a lot of attention to the culture side of things. If our culture starts atrophying, our online presence is going to reflect that, and who is going to want to do business with that company? You're just another factory as far as I am concerned."

Factories are boring.

When customer service is valued by everyone in an organization, there will be no responsibility silos and the customer will win. This starts with integrating customer service into every job description. Jenny continues, "Customers expect help. It has to be fundamental to your culture that you cannot resent the fact that someone is asking you to do your job. If you are in a position to help somebody, you are obligated to help and ask for help if you need it. We focus very much on making that culture internal so that the behaviors are expressed externally."

When everyone understands what the mission is, scripting is not required. If it is in line with what we are trying to accomplish, there needs to be some latitude to get creative. Customers can tell when something is scripted. We've all made calls that were outsourced to call centers. The people who work at these centers are bound by whatever approved conversations they have been provided.

When life is unscripted, however, there are gray areas.

You Say Stalking; We Say Proactive Gesturing

As mentioned previously, the wealth of insights found in unsolicited brand mentions within social channels can be enlightening. So the question becomes, what do we do with this information? We touch on exploring the boundaries in Chapter 4, "Character in 140 Characters." Perhaps terms like "customer engagement innovators" or "customer experience innovators" would be more appropriate than "customer stalkers." There can be a positive connotation to stalking, however, if it includes caring enough to listen effectively and to provide a personalized experience.

On one hand, if it's public, then it's fair game. This doesn't mean that it would be appropriate to share or rebroadcast everything that is found, but users shouldn't be surprised when businesses start to take action on the public content they post. Connecting the virtual dots to create an experience may require some extra effort, but it will not go unnoticed and can yield extraordinary results.

More often than not, proactively following Twitter users in the Manhattan area has resulted in a positive response and many times unexpected results from both parties. The public and real-time nature of Twitter allows us to catch some folks near or within a Tasti D-Lite location on a regular basis. One such connection was made early in 2009 with Rick Liebling (then @eyecube on Twitter, now @Rick_Now). An alert on the term "Empire State Building" let us know one day that he worked in the building. After following him on Twitter and doing a little research, we posted the following on the main Tasti D-Lite account:

Tasti D-Lite
@tastidlite

@eyecube Love your blog. http://bit.ly/4ffc Stop by downstairs and bring a friend. http://bit.ly/F08d Enjoy!

Enjoy!: A proactive gesture. How would Rick respond?

This unsolicited gesture provided a link to a BOGO (buy one, get one free) coupon in our Empire State Building location and also promoted Rick's blog which showed that we at least took the time to find it and take a look at it. This was a little risky perhaps given that Rick had 600 followers at the time. Here was his response:

Rick Liebling
@eyecube

@tastidlite – You rock. Got some big Tastidlite fans in our office. Will be down shortly.

The response: To be fair, you can throw a rock in Manhattan and hit a Tasti D-Lite fan.

We were able to see that four people had clicked on the link that was sent. Our point-of-sale system verified his visit through the redemption of the unique coupon code. Later, he posted this:

Rick Liebling
@eyecube

@tastidlite – thanks again. The Banada Fudge was good. Liked the consistency.

Follow-up: Rick lets us know about his visit.

While we were thrilled with his response, we wanted to take the experience to the next level. Through his blog we were able to discover the name of his company, and we had our associates take a cake and some other frozen Tasti treats to his office and surprise him as a way of saying thanks.

Rick Liebling
@eyecube

@tastidlite just came up to my office, game me gobs of amazing treats as a thank you. Tastidlites pwns me now.

Surprise: Amazing treats for everyone!

Rick would later write in his blog, "That day I was the hero of the office. Everyone wanted to know how I got these, and I probably told the story 10 times."

His perspective on the experience? "Here's where TastiDlite really took it to the next level. Now, I've got a face (or two) to put with the story. Now, when I go downstairs to TastiDlite, I've got two friends. They've been to my place of business; they've given me something tangible. How many of you can say that about your Twitter/Facebook/Blog friends? No matter how engaging and transparent we are online, it's no match for face-to-face engagement."[4]

Many of Rick's office mates also joined the Twitter discussion and others would learn about Tasti D-Lite as a result of Rick sharing his experience.

Alyssa Ando
@andoa

Finally got to try @tastidlite after reading about it through @eyecube. A walk through Central Park with choc mousse sundae. Mmmm!

Mmmm: Word of mouth can be yummy.

Rick no longer works in the Empire State Building, but we recently tracked him down at marketing and communications firm Y&R New York where he holds the title creative culturist.

In later chapters we talk about what it takes to execute on what should be simple campaigns like this. Processes and protocols aside, the human requirements are what they are. Human.

Be Human and Tell a Story

As long as there have been humans communicating, we've used stories to relate to each other, make sense of the world around us, and help us make decisions as we go through life. Changes in technology have us sharing greater amounts of information, and we're finding ourselves making more decisions based on those stories.

If having great ideas and remarkable testimony enables anyone to have a voice in this new socially empowered world, then the future has much to offer when it comes to corporate storytelling and brand journalism.

This rise of "brand journalism" was included among the top 12 trends in public relations for 2012 by the Public Relations Society of America (PRSA).[5] Many corporations looking to hire talent in this area are starting to connect with journalists coming out of the declining print industries.

The role of companies has changed. Being publishers of corporate stories and content that will educate and help shape perception of the brand has moved us away from earned or pitched media to owned media; that real estate on the web that brands own and control.

Thomas Scott is a franchise friend and CEO of Brand Journalists, a Nashville, Tennessee–based firm that provides PR, social media, blogging, and organic SEO services for franchise systems. He offers some background on this growing industry:

> Brand journalism involves telling stories about a company that makes readers want to know more, stories that don't read like marketing or advertising copy. It means having conversations with them—not preaching at them and giving them real and interesting stories they can relate to.
>
> People today are so inundated with advertising and marketing speak they now filter out marketing messages. I believe that humans, adults in particular, first judge things as relevant. Before they'll listen to what you have to communicate, there's a filter that says either (a) it's relevant to what I'm interested in or (b) it's really not relevant and I don't care. There's no in between on that. When it comes to being marketed to, consumers have these filters more pronounced than ever. So the only

way to cut through the noise is to get yourself in the relevant bucket.

You do that by telling stories. The story is the essence of human communication and as long as humans have communicated, we have used stories to make sense of the world around us, help us relate to each other and to help us make decisions.

As humans we're wired with a desire to make a human connection. This might explain why when someone is telling you a good story, you don't even realize it. That's the power of a well-told story. It allows the company or organization to become human. Thomas says, "Being human is about having a real, honest connection with people. There's a real promise with social media and the conversational and emotional connections with people that can happen there." We talk more about the importance of brand stories in Chapter 8, "Brand Stewardship."

So where do we find these storytellers, and where do they belong on the organizational chart? We speak in Chapter 3, "Going Behind the Brand," about the next generation of digital natives who may know the tools but don't have the business acumen. Here the issue is the lack of good storytelling skills. Thomas says, "I will say that while young people understand the tools and know what is relevant, they simply lack the life experience. The older people are more likely to have the stories as well as the storytelling skills."

With the failures in banking and the stock market, customers are looking for businesses they can trust and feel good about. Thomas continues, "In today's marketplace, attraction trumps promotion. This approach builds trust and distinguishes a company from its competitors. The message is more important than the money. People need to tell better stories. It doesn't really matter if you're a large company or a small company. To me, it is really an equalizer. In this age of technology where we're all connected, you can't fake the message."

The Heart of the Matter

Constant pursuit of relevance should be our objective. Bigger budgets won't buy anything in today's world of democratized search results. Being human will truly be more effective, but how will that happen in our highly scripted and process-oriented businesses?

Perhaps our stalking example in this chapter will reinforce the point that a customer experience strategy needs to start with paying attention. With trust and customer confidence on the line, lasting results will come only when we're actively and intentionally engaging in ways that are relevant, and human.

Everyone has a story to tell. Share yours, and see what happens.

CHAPTER 6

You Can't Outsource Relationships

> Little happens in a relationship until the individuals learn to trust each other.
>
> —*David W. Johnson, author and emeritus professor, University of Minnesota*

The age-old debate continues. Do we outsource, or keep it in-house? Throw social media into that query, and you'll get some lively discussion. With so many new channels in use by consumers to connect with businesses, who has the time to add social functions on top of already busy and overworked call centers, sales desks, and support reps? Many organizations are overwhelmed when it comes to meeting consumers where they are in this new frontier, but as we've seen, this opportunity is exceptional and well worth the investment.

The feasibility of putting these relationships in the hands of a third party will vary depending on the type of business. Most people agree that long term there will be a greater integration within existing corporate disciplines and core business functions when these things are not outsourced. For now, many are opting just to write a check each month to deal with these types of activities, but this can come at great risk. We've met some very effective digital agencies over the last few years, but we have also seen some that are simply taking advantage of unwary marketers and business owners. This wave of new opportunities has many people just wanting to get a piece of the action by offering automated and canned solutions for as long as they can get away with it.

This chapter reviews the risks and potential benefits of using a third party to manage various business activities related to these new social opportunities. Again, organizational size, type, and structure will play a significant part in these decisions. We intend to show here that there are fundamental differences in approach and mindset that have serious and long-term implications for businesses of all kinds. If you are in it to win, you had better get this one right because it's all about the most important asset that you have—relationships.

Consider the activities related to the traditional sales funnel. At each point and beyond, there are opportunities to delegate or hand off the management of certain functions such as driving awareness, engagement, or customer service after the sale. With the advent of social media, the mouth of the sales funnel just got a whole lot bigger, and the tasks of listening or the monitoring function have grown along with it. This is where we start.

How Well Can You Listen?

At this point, you should understand that the wealth of information found in online communities can and should be considered valuable business intelligence. Leaving the monitoring to an outsourced partner could easily cause an organization to miss out on rich customer insights and direct feedback. Additionally, if the voice of the customer is embraced as part of the brand culture and that voice is not heard accurately, there may be a disconnect with those providing the goods or services. Any misalignment can lead to unmet expectations for both parties. Understanding the customer perspective within an organization becomes difficult if the message is being relayed through others.

This is reminiscent of the whisper game in which participants in a group attempt to convey a message all the way around a circle only to find that the end result is a complete departure from the original statement. When your customers are speaking, what are you really hearing and how many people or processes are between you and the customer? The company that is closest to the consumer will win every time.

With that said, listening effectively requires time and energy. Allowing a third party to manage monitoring and information gathering applications could be an efficient way to glean only the critical data you require. Consolidated social intelligence on trends, sentiment, survey results, and feedback reports provided by an agency would help in making operational, marketing, and customer service decisions, assuming that the information is utilized properly.

An entire industry has been formed around capturing, measuring, and selling the vast amounts of consumer data now on the web. Sophisticated software solutions can be expensive if they are purchased outright. An agency partner could share the financial load of such software among other clients. Aside from the terabytes of raw data available, conversational context could contain other insights invaluable to a business owner. Whether handled internally or managed by a third party, capturing and reporting this information is critical. There are many great stories to be found and shared, but these conversations could get lost if they are filtered through some automated monitoring software. The context of these stories needs to be understood; even the anecdotal can bring great insights to light.

Making Contact

New ways to drive brand awareness and connect with consumers using these media are unfolding every day. Businesses are positioning themselves to take advantage of these opportunities, but is this really anything new? The medium may be different, but the root of the outsourcing issue is one that has been around for decades.

Some years ago at Mail Boxes Etc. the need arose to handle a significant number of inbound inquiries for franchise development. The decision to outsource a phone bank to handle the thousands of leads that were coming in each year was not an easy one. Postimplementation, it was learned that not only did the lead quality decrease, but continuity went down, and the closing ratios went down over time as well. Ultimately the outsourcing was discontinued. The reality is that every time you put a layer or barrier in between you and the customer, you are creating more opportunities for miscommunication and failure. There is no substitute for person-to-person communication. As soon as the baton is handed off for that initial consumer connection, the most crucial element of the business—namely, the relationship—is in someone else's hands. No one knows more about your company than those people who are vested in the process, and no one has a more profound understanding of what is happening internally with the product or service.

Particular caution should be taken to the first, and what is often the most poignant, contact with potential customers as there is no second chance at impacting that first touch point. If credibility does not transfer effectively between two parties, the rest of the relationship will be impacted as a result.

When you outsource, it not only affects the initial contact, but it lengthens the time or opportunity you have to form the relationship and deepen it. If time kills deals, it would seem important to establish a level of trust from the outset. You have to be very thoughtful about outsourcing any relationship that is important to you.

Who's Engaging Your Customer?

For the sake of this discussion, we consider engagement to cover sales support, customer service, and general interaction. Interaction with customers happens every day at the line level in the physical realm, and over the years both online and offline feedback mechanisms have been developed to gain important insights. We've since perfected the associated routing processes through mail, e-mail, and so on to be distributed to the appropriate party. Online interactions however are much more dynamic and candid, and they take place in real time. These conversations could consist of anything from simple brand mentions, sales, or support inquiries to complaints and customer service issues, any of which can be shared in full view of the community with potential viral consequences.

To show the level of attention and agility required online these days, consider the following, which was posted in June 2011 by Ashton Kutcher, who at the time had just over 7 million followers on Twitter:

@aplusk
ashton kutcher

Hey @AmericanAir are you aware that you are advertising on a site that supports the Sale of Human Beings (slavery?)

Slavery?: Ashton Kutcher reaches out to American Airlines.

Without going into the details of such a report, imagine the discipline required to properly address this in a timely manner in just the right way to avoid a potential disaster. Now imagine that your response is in the hands of a third party potentially disconnected from the resources required to fix the problem.

Within 13 minutes, American Airlines responded with this:

@AmericanAir
American Airlines

@aplusk We will address this IMMEDIATELY. Can you please DM us detail of the site, including a link?

The response: American Airlines responds within 13 minutes.

Three hours later, this tweet brought the conversation to an end:

@aplusk
ashton kutcher

Thank you! Via dm @AmericanAir --> Heads up: Ads should be down w/in the hour. Blank ads are being served for now.

Thank you!: Ashton let's everyone know how American Airlines is resolving the issue.

Literally, anything at any time can surface online around a brand or business. With all the possible variables, channel management can be a complex animal to conquer. Many brands segment these functions into different online accounts that are managed separately.

Take for example Verizon which manages no less than 20 separate accounts on Twitter catering to different needs related to its products. Within its wireless arm alone, you'll find @VerizonWireless, @VZWNetwork, @CareersAtVZW, and @VZWSupport. Customers could subscribe to or follow and engage with only the feed in which they have interest and is relevant to them.

So the question is who is having these conversations with your customers? Experts or not, a third party may not be close enough to the daily action or the resources found within the corporate office.

We mention the timing element in Chapter 1. More layers can mean more delays and longer reaction times. As fast as things can go wrong online, precious minutes could be wasted on red tape and complex communication protocols.

As difficult as this may sound, business has always had a way of creating partner industries to help augment all kinds of specific marketing and support functions. The rise of social technologies is no different. In fact, digital agencies of all kinds are growing rapidly as businesses reach out for help now more than ever. Could a specialty firm do a better job than the internal teams? That's a decision only you can make. An outside perspective can sometimes see the big picture and tie together cross-discipline activities with specialized staff dedicated to meeting these needs with the possible exception of the sales discipline. Sophisticated social CRM software can potentially tie together contacts and conversations even across channels to provide a better customer experience online. Additionally, outside agencies are typically better at measuring ROI because they are expected to deliver it where internally the temptation could be that it is just part of the job.

Tasti D-Lite area developer Bill Warshaw works with a local firm to help manage his social efforts. When asked about the depth of the relationship, he offers, "It was key that they understand the business as well as anybody could because they were going to help communicate our message to the public." Bill stays in tune with customer feedback through regular activity and campaign reports. Over time, the Facebook and Twitter activity has been able to synchronize well with the main Tasti D-Lite profiles, promoting and interacting with each other frequently.

Outsourcing Your Voice

Following or "liking" a brand on a social network allows a consumer to get closer to the brand than ever before with more access to information and (hopefully) a direct connection to the heart and voice of the brand. But who will meet them there? Handing over the responsibility of communicating that voice and message comes with great risk. Whether it's a first-time engagement with a potential customer or with one who has been a loyal fan for years, having integrity with the messaging and consistency of the brand voice across multiple social channels can provide another competitive advantage.

Over the last several years, brand presence online has become a vital component of marketing a business. With more possible touch points with consumers, representation of the personality and voice of those behind the product or service has to be consistent across many channels simultaneously. Put into the hands of others, this critical element of communicating culture can be difficult at best and disastrous at worst.

Our outsourcing risk versus benefit summary below provides pros and cons of outsourcing in the areas of listening, engagement, and messaging.

Outsourcing Risk Versus Benefit Summary

	LISTENING	ENGAGEMENT	MESSAGING
RISK	Potential loss of valuable business intelligence	Not directly in touch with those behind the brand who are empowered to resolve issues	Potential miscommunication of brand voice and culture
BENEFIT	Access to expensive monitoring software with consolidated reporting	The use of a social CRM platform by an agency could help provide a better customer experience	More consistent brand messaging across channels

At the end of the day, this is about communication. Adding an additional layer between the customer and the business could threaten relationships and eventually profits.

Do Customers Care?

From the customers' perspective, knowing that they are able to connect directly and quickly to decision makers and those closest to the products and services they use and love is an obvious benefit. In today's technology-driven marketplace, this may be the only advantage and distinction an organization has. The company that is the closest to the customer has no competition.

Being able to get to know some of the faces behind the now fading corporate veil personalizes the experience. Rosanna Fiske, CEO of the Public Relations Society of America offers this: "Ultimately, it comes down to business outcomes. The focus shouldn't be on who 'owns' social media, but rather, how it can be deployed most successfully across an organization." That could include agency partners already effectively managing other customer-facing elements such as direct marketing, advertising, and public relations among others.

Customers certainly care if they are violated. There is considerable opportunity to offend a consumer when you are passing relationships between people. You leave yourself wide open to misunderstandings and unmet expectations, and you put yourself in the position of delivering on someone else's promises. As the business scales up, so will the issues. The most important relationship you have is the one with the customer. The effective management of that relationship is clearly your responsibility.

Masking Transparency

This discussion deserves a "can't" versus "won't" evaluation. In other words, not being able to manage things internally is different from not wanting to. Some organizations cannot manage customer online actions internally because of a lack of scale or even too much scale; others may not have the culture to support it.

Smaller companies may have the passion and desire to manage all these elements, but they often do not have the talent to support them. Developing a proper content strategy and providing a consistent brand voice becomes difficult when there are no dedicated resources.

On the other hand, if a business chooses not to manage these relationships in-house because the culture is prohibitive, you have bigger problems. If an agency can do it better because it is not hindered by the corporate culture, then it may be time to take a hard look in the mirror. Much of this goes back to the culture conversation. Does your company culture support this kind of transparency? Would an agency simply be a mask intended to make your business appear transparent?

If the culture and the values are such that they won't tolerate transparency or open-book management, then having a customer relationship at the beginning isn't going to make a difference. A business can actually be successful with a sterile growth pattern that is solely based on infrastructure, systems, and metrics, but the true trajectories take place when you have real people helping real people and when this help involves emotion and connection and understanding. These components are vital if you want dynamic and exponential growth, and this won't happen without the human elements.

There are obvious opportunities and reasons to choose to outsource, but you have to work very hard to make sure that the connections reflect your culture and core values and that they become human, emotional, and effective touch points in some way. The challenge then becomes establishing and managing a relationship with those who are a proxy for your relationship with the consumer or the people you are trying to touch. You have to formulate an incentive to make them willing to be trained so you can inculcate your values and culture to the people who are going to have the initial contact with the consumer. But even if they get it initially, you can't pass the baton of trust to someone else. You can't mandate relationships to a third party, and you can't transfer intimacy.

This doesn't mean that businesses and organizations won't be successful, but it does mean that the outcome can be very clinical and mechanical. There won't be any exuberance or emotion associated with it or the long-term ability to maintain the relationship unless you own it yourself. And ownership of that relationship may be the one thing that sets a business apart from its competitors and delivers sustainability in the future.

When Things Go Wrong

Outsourced third parties typically have other accounts they are managing for customer service, support, and engagement. Over time, there have been incidents where mishaps have occurred when inappropriate content was published ultimately exposing the fact that the social initiatives were being outsourced. The real challenge for the brand is handling the potential fallout from such an incident. The response will speak volumes to the members of the community and will often leave an impression greater than the initial blunder.

When the F bomb was dropped within the Chrysler Twitter stream in March 2011 to 7,000 followers, it was quickly revealed that the misfire was caused by an individual at an agency hired to help manage the account.

Chrysler Autos
@Chrysler Autos

I find it ironic that Detroit is known as the #motorcity and yet no one here knows how to f****** drive

#Motorcity: The infamous Chrysler F bomb.

Before the post could be deleted, a number of Chrysler's Twitter followers forwarded the curious message to all of their followers thus extending the reach of the colorful tweet. What was intended as a personal message unfortunately turned into a PR issue which left Chrysler with some important decisions to make. There is no undo button in these kinds of situations. Clearly the agency needs to help with damage control, but does it simply become the scapegoat or at least in this case a protective layer insulating the client from full responsibility? Regardless of the initial offense, the next move by the brand would speak volumes to the offended Twitter community. Should the post be deleted, would there be an apology and an explanation, or would there be an attempt at a cover-up? Should the agency be dismissed, or is there an apology (or even a laugh) and everyone moves on?

Many times it is not the actual blunder or even the fact that a third party was responsible that is the problem. It's the overall response of the brand that is often carefully scrutinized by the community. In other words, the spirit of the response is looked upon as more important than the mistakes. It is with this response that the intent and motive are exposed. Even if handled internally, these kinds of mishaps can and do occur, possibly with terrible outcomes.

Turning over these responsibilities to a third party has both risks and benefits. Just because there are resources available for just about any specialized activity to help, doesn't mean they should be utilized.

The two directional approaches that we have reviewed here are allowing culture and messaging to come from the inside out, and managing a third party to push insights and relationships from the outside in. As we've seen, each approach has its own challenges and outcomes. If done internally, intimacy with the customer remains intact. Relationships are handled directly by those working within the disciplines that serve them. Insights and the virtual perspective become part of the corporate DNA more easily and more naturally. Where third parties are managing parts of the relationship, transferring those insights and that intimacy can be difficult. If outsourced, how does the information become integrated into other parts of the enterprise? How do the social CRM data make their way into customer service, operations, or manufacturing for example? If the objective is to remove layers and get closer to customers, closing that gap should be a priority before your competitors seize the opportunity.

Questions to Consider

Whether you are already outsourcing social activities or assessing your needs as you manage your social activities internally, answering the following questions may help you move the needle toward customer intimacy:

1. Do you feel out of touch with your customer? Could you make better decisions with direct access to more information? How many layers are between you and your customer?
2. Are you hearing anecdotal stories of online interaction related to your business? If so, how many other stories might you be missing?
3. Are your core business functions and disciplines integrating social components? If not, why?
4. Is your brand being represented online with an authentic and accurate voice? Is it aligned with your culture, mission, and values?
5. What relationship touch points are you passing off to others? Is this acceptable to you?

Our friend Thomas Scott, CEO of Brand Journalists, sees a lot of brand and agency relationships:

What I see working in other agencies is a bit of a hybrid. We have a team approach for social media where there are people in the organization who handle some of the engagement. Maybe they can't focus on it all the time, so we monitor it and produce content and push it out. We make sure if there's something they need to respond to, they get on it. They're also interacting and driving content. That works really well and really takes off when you do it that way. You may have five or six admins on a Facebook page and maybe three or four people who have access to Twitter. It's kind of a joint effort. That seems to work better because it addresses the lack of skills and what the company has and still gives them control and access.

The Heart of the Matter

Social media should be more than a budget line item. Abdicating the responsibility of customer relationships to others who don't have a vested interest in the business is a tragic decision. While this has always been the case, it applies even more so in the new economy and business environment we find ourselves in.

CHAPTER 7

Rolling with the Big Boys

The ability to learn faster than
your competitors may be the only
sustainable competitive advantage.
—*Arie de Geus, Head of Planning, Royal Dutch Shell*

Being competitive in a land of giants used to require really great ideas and deep pockets. While the Internet has served as an equalizer of sorts and the playing field is being leveled, the game is still on and the stakes are higher than ever. Good ideas are still required, but good stories are just as likely, if not more likely, to make an impact. Punching above your weight class in this environment has less to do with attacking the competition than with pursuing the hearts of customers. As you'll see, however, having your people and platforms in place is a big part of the contest.

Making an Early Splash

On today's web, just about any size business can make a big splash at the right time if done in the right way. Being an early adopter in a new online community, for example, can make you look like a bigger fish because the pond is smaller in the beginning. As the pond grows however, major brands and larger early players will start crowding the space and start to demand more attention. Getting there first can help secure a foothold and establish a solid brand presence with fans and followers. As the buzz around the application or social network grows, businesses creating remarkable customer experiences will be included within the conversation. Couple this with the opportunity to make valuable media connections within those communities, and interesting things will happen.

Our early efforts to engage customers in new ways online began to get the attention of others watching the trends. This resulted in Tasti D-Lite's first mention in Mashable via their 40 of the Best Twitter Brands and the People Behind Them list in January 2009. With names like Ford, Best Buy, and Starbucks on the roster, our inclusion in this early list propelled us into a "ones to watch" class and seemed to help fuel and amplify our future efforts. It is interesting to note that there was only one other company on the list that had fewer followers than we did at the time.[1]

These types of mentions have generated a significant amount of awareness for the Tasti D-Lite brand name within the various channels. The attention continues to feed on itself to this day and snowballs with each campaign and article or blog post.

Sanderson and Associates helps Tasti D-Lite and Planet Smoothie with public relations efforts here in the United States. We asked the president, Rhonda Sanderson, how she saw smaller companies leveraging social media to drive brand awareness. She responded, "To a smaller business, particularly a food service business, social media is like the ultimate blessing dropped by the marketing gods. For those who really can't afford a decent advertising or media campaign, social media is the one tool that can help them reach out to their customer and develop an online personality that their clientele can relate to."

Getting started and establishing an active presence does at least two things. First, and perhaps most important, if consumers know that a brand is listening, they will likely reach out directly in the event of a customer service need. Instead of broadcasting their cry to the entire community, hopefully they'll try the direct route first and give the business a chance to respond and address those concerns quickly and relatively quietly. Second, if they know that a business is participating, users will be more likely to include the brand user name or identifier in the conversations, which will make others aware of the brand presence. We touch on this in Chapter 4, "Character in 140 Characters."

Social Anxiety

Let's be honest. We all look at the numbers and want to have more fans or followers than the next person. For the business owner, boosting those numbers can alleviate the anxiety that comes with comparing oneself with the nearest competitor. After all, looking at a healthy online profile of a competitor can be rather intimidating. This very real concern plays into the social pysche that we all deal with as we evaluate our digital presence. Rather than this viral envy, what we should really be concerned about is the substance behind the numbers; the quality of engagement, and reach and impact. As we mention in Chapter 2, "The Race for Transparency," the active and robust presence of a competitor online may discourage some people from entering the space altogether and throw in the towel before they even start. Watching a rival trying to interact and meet the needs of your customers will motivate you one way or another. When the competitor gets a lot of great press for that engagement, it adds insult to injury.

To add to the anxiety, any attempt at simply copying the online efforts of others will many times demonstrate a lack of uniqueness and the authenticity that consumers are looking for.

Eyes on the Prize

Is it more important to focus on what competitors are doing or what consumers are doing online? As it relates to building trust and loyalty, clearly the latter is going to yield the insights you need to best meet the needs of customers. With so much information to gather on the open web, how much time and energy should be spent watching? At worst, fixating on the latest moves by competitors can serve as a distraction and paralyze you while you scramble to keep up with whatever new solutions they are implementing. But how do you know if these shiny new toys are right for your customers and your brand? Only trial and error and hands on engagement will lead to the kind of customer intimacy we are all looking for. Again, this takes us back to the mountain illustration we use in Chapter 1, "Introduction to a Tasti Story." Shortcuts to the top will not yield the real experience needed for what comes next. What we gain through doing the hard work will support us going forward. At the end of the day, the value of the journey matters.

Again, trying to replicate the efforts of another business carries certain risks. For one, empowered consumers can spot a counterfeit a mile away. If your online profile screams, "Me, too," then you're doing something wrong.

Being the business that is being copied can be quite irritating. We've seen competitors try to replicate our campaigns to the point where customers wonder if Tasti D-Lite and the other brand are related. This kind of activity can make you want to shut down. It can also serve as a distraction and take the focus off of what is really important.

It goes without saying that being clueless when it comes to what the competition is doing is not good business. However, with the needs of the marketplace changing so rapidly, being consumed with what the competition is doing means paying less attention to customers. Getting out of step with them is not something you can afford to do for very long in this economy. You can either chase your customers or chase your competition. Following customers will never lead you into a hole or brick wall.

This is not a sprint; it is a marathon. The difference here is that there is no finish line; it is instead a continuous journey. Outexecuting and outlasting competitors require discipline and perseverance. Even if there is an end to one social network, another opportunity will replace it. Opportunities will continually shift as communities grow and new technologies emerge. Innovating at the point when an opportunity emerges is one of the keys to staying competitive and relevant online.

Can't Buy Me Love, but What About Likes?

Competing online means that the numbers are out there for everyone to see. Fans, followers, likes, views, subscribers, comments, shares, and such have become the accepted units of measurement for popularity. Factors contributing to these numbers can include the age of the business, time invested online, the number of retail units, demographics, and many other variables. Is it true that if business X has more "likes" than business Y on Facebook then business X is more reputable and more successful and has more brand equity? How much of this is a true reflection of the offline world, and is it possible to skew reality one way or another? While services such as Klout and industry indexes like the Restaurant Social Media Index are developing models that are based on the measurement of influence and online engagement, numbers still carry a lot of weight and contribute greatly to a brand's perception of credibility. The question is, are we looking at a network of connections that is simply a mile wide and an inch deep? Are fewer strong connections more valuable than many weak ones, or does the real opportunity exist somewhere in the middle?

As it turns out, acquiring at least the appearance of a great social following isn't that hard to achieve. You can buy just about anything online today including an artificial presence. The following are real auction descriptions and associated buy-it-now prices that we found on eBay:

> "10,000 unique views to your YouTube channel, $9.95"
>
> "1000 Facebook Likes! REAL Human Facebook likes to your fan page guaranteed, $23.95"
>
> "Buy 5000 targeted Twitter Followers (in 20 days), $24.99"
>
> "100 verifiable Blog Comments on your Website, $11.95"

Alternatively (and so convenient), one could purchase an account preloaded with followers:

> "Buy pre-made TWITTER PAGE with 2000 Unique Real Followers, $6.95"

Sounds like a bargain, doesn't it? Why not skip all the hard work and save time and money by paying a nominal fee to kick-start your social media presence? Not so fast. As is true in the real world, it turns out in the digital world that there is no shortcut to success either.

In fact, entire business models are being created around fan and follower acquisition for online business profiles. One such company boasts on its FAQs (frequently asked questions) page: "We have performed on orders of up to 1 million fans."[2]

Apparently there is more than one way to skin a cat when it comes to targeted advertising within social networks. Beyond the structured and recognized methods that each platform provides, an enormous gray area exists where enterprising companies are taking advantage of those feeling pressured to have large numbers of fans and followers. Could this work for certain types of businesses? Are some of the solutions offered legitimate? Of course, but just what exactly are you paying for and what are you receiving? Building an authentic online brand presence should start with real numbers.

As we have already mentioned, one of the arguments for desiring high fan and follower counts is to break through the perception issues that exist not only for potential customers but for the business owner and competitors as well. It would seem logical that customers would be more likely to commit to a connection when a business profile has a large number of followers rather than just a few. Perhaps there is safety in numbers when it comes to joining a conversation online. Does this mean that those following the crowd are potentially less committed? And how does trust play into this numbers game? Seeing the difference between substance and fluff is not difficult. We are all consumers after all.

Boris Pluskowski is senior vice president of innovation strategy at Spigit, a software company that allows organizations to crowd source ideas and innovation by reaching out and engaging customers and associates in reinventing the core and thereby creating value in the company. About these numbers he says, "Engaging audiences in meaningless conversation that doesn't achieve anything is a pointless activity. Ultimately, if you go out and you get a ton of 'likes' on your Facebook page, what does that really give you? Perhaps some notional marketing here and there, but how does that actually translate to real value for the company? It's very difficult to quantify."

Inflating community numbers with accounts that do not have genuine patrons or at least potential customers just for the sake of numbers can carry some risks, not the least of which is a breach of integrity and trust:

1. Having subscribers who are not familiar with your product or service could bring some awkward posts with inane questions or inappropriate replies.
2. If, in fact, the accounts are real people but not the target demographic, over time they will lose interest and drop out thus causing numbers to decrease and offsetting any organic growth brought by real customers. If they are not really potential customers to begin with, why would they contribute to or demonstrate a real interest in your products or services?
3. If exposed, acquiring fans or followers in a questionable manner will not be received well by the community.

Here are some questions to ask yourself:

1. Would having a large following within a given social network simply be providing you with false comfort?
2. How do you plan to sustain the community even if the numbers are there?
3. Are you simply giving in to social envy? Knee-jerk reactions will get flash-in-the-pan results at best.

The Value of Organic Growth

One of the concepts in the business of obtaining likes and followers for businesses is Blumpo. On the Blumpo website FAQs page, we found this:

Q: *Will the fans start leaving after your service has finished?*
A: Not at all, our fans are real people and are active Facebook users. If you give them regular interesting content, then they will stay. You have to manage them just like e-mail marketing. Don't spam them, don't always sell, and create a relationship with them."[3]

Hidden TreatCard Fun

Determining the level of response can be done in some creative ways. In December 2009, we held a little experiment that yielded some encouraging results. For two days, we gave followers on Twitter notice that we would be posting a video on a certain day and time that would reveal the location of a hidden $50 TreatCard at a Tasti D-Lite location somewhere in New York City.

Skyler Fox
@beefyfunk

pandemonion! RT @tastidlite: CHECK THIS OUT: Tom night @ 8pm we will reveal the location of a $50 TreatCard hidden somewhere in Manhattan

Pandemonium!: Skyler Fox comments
on our hidden TreatCard idea.

The link to the video would come via a tweet at the specified time. Whoever was following along on Twitter and watched the video would have the opportunity to get to the location first and claim the hidden gift card. We had no idea just how long it would take for someone to arrive or how many people would show up. As it turned out, we didn't have to watch the clock for long because just seven minutes after the video was posted, Virginia arrived asking if anyone had claimed the card yet. She knew where to look and walked out with the card. Afterwards, she posted this:

Virginia Zint
@naneenya

Just won a $50 TreatCard to @tastidlite !! It pays to be on Twitter!

The winner!: Virginia shares with her friends.

Once we announced that the card had been found, no one else arrived to claim it. There are certainly easier ways to find out if customers are listening, but this was a fun test of follower engagement.

(Note: We have to give credit to the country music duo Sugarland who have been known to do something similar with sold-out concert tickets. We borrowed the idea from them.)

Going Deep and Local

Local businesses continue to struggle with the presence of big box retailers in many markets. The ability to connect with customers online around very specific local market needs and events is starting to show promise. Drilling down into a community and the happenings within are resulting in deeper connections with many of these businesses that are just starting online.

Bill Warshaw is owner of the Tasti D-Lite in Times Square in New York City. With much to distract potential customers in the theater district, Bill has managed to not only forge valuable connections with other local businesses, but he has managed to take those conversations online. Bill says, "As a franchisee, it's very important to stay local and work with other businesses and people in the area to build support. By using social media, you have that ability to engage them that much faster and easier, and you see results faster."

Broadway show ticket raffles and giveaways often include special flavor names and product offerings to go along with the theme of the musicals that Bill partners with. Actors make appearances to meet customers, and then photos are shared online. The interaction between the Times Square Tasti D-Lite Twitter and Facebook accounts and the musical helps build the buzz and attract new customers. Bill says, "The theaters will send out blasts letting them [customers] know of the Tasti D-Lite promotion so they can come in with their ticket stub, get a discount, and try the special flavor we created." He continues, "People write in and say how happy they are that we are engaged in the local area and the theater."

This should take us back to the conversation on the unique benefits of franchising and social media from Chapter 2, "The Race for Transparency." Local ownership equipped with these digital tools can be a powerful thing in the marketplace and can have a micro (local) as well as macro (global) influence on the marketplace. "Going viral" is no longer dependent on size, scale, or location. It has everything to do with making an impact on customers and meeting the needs of the marketplace in new ways.

Ready at the Line

The real chemistry, relationship, and connection with fans or followers need to translate into value at the line level and have an influence on unit economics. Otherwise the numbers mean nothing and are much like thunder and lightning but no rain. There has to be meaningful results. Big box or mom-and-pop enterprises, everything goes back to unit economics and execution on the front lines.

Engaging customers in different ways online is one thing. Interacting with them around new technologies will require not only preparation but more, as we discuss in Chapter 9, "The Location Business." Until such time as technology matures and our adoption becomes widespread, we'll most likely need to work through a variety of mechanics and protocols. One example may be self-serve checkout registers at grocery stores; awkward at first, but convenient for the most part if you are the type who would rather deal with technology than people.

In the early days of location-based marketing, we started experimenting with mobile coupons on Twitter that simply required customers to show us the coupon on their phone to redeem it at the location mentioned.

Tasti D-Lite
@tastidlite

MOBILE COUPON: Show/print this msg for a 99 CENT SMALL Tasti D-Lite CUP OR CONE only at Columbus Circle NYC. Expires 8/1/09

Mobile coupon: An early example of using
Twitter for distributing mobile offers.

Within these 140 characters is an entire campaign targeting those who were following our Twitter account, many of whom at the time were in New York City. Associates at the counter would need to be able to recognize the offer and record the redemption. While it took us some time and energy to gain the following on Twitter, the campaign cost nothing from an advertising perspective.

One advantage smaller organizations have is being able to quickly train those who are to be involved in this kind of transaction. Having those individuals ready ahead of the technology curve is one way to stay out in front of the big guys. The clear risk for anyone doing this is that any disconnect between the online presence and store personnel can ruin both the online experience and the face-to-face experience for the customer.

Location-based services and mobile applications have now made these kinds of offers mainstream at the retail level, and awareness on both sides of the counter is much higher. The business tools available to manage these kinds of campaigns make scaling across a network and enterprise much easier. We talk more about location-based marketing in Chapter 9, "The Location Business."

Think about what it would take in your organization to execute a simple campaign like the mobile coupon example above, and ask yourself these questions:

1. Would you need approval from the legal department? If so, what would that involve?
2. Who would decide what kind of offers would be effective?

3. Would you need to go through communications, market-ing, or someone else to actually publish the offer?
4. How many layers within the operations department would you need to go through to get the information to the front lines?
5. Who would you need to help track redemptions at the point of sale so you could measure the results?

Now total up the number of people who would have to be involved in doing something like this. If your number is more than three, your organization may have some streamlining to do if you are serious about keeping up with the competition.

Getting the Platform Ready

Personnel and processes are just part of the equation when it comes to leadership in the marketplace. Having the right tech-nologies in place to power even the smallest of social enterprises means having effective systems and applications standardized across a network.

We asked David Gosman, CEO of point-of-sale vendor pcAmerica about his perspective on the value of this kind of platform:

> It's very difficult when you have different, fragmented systems out in the field. If you have three disparate systems in your organization, you have to reinvent the wheel three times to make sure that your technology goals can be met at all locations. You may be restricted from certain initiatives because one or more of those systems can't accomplish what you're looking to do. Your goals of rolling out a franchisewide initiative will be limited as some locations won't be able to participate.

From a customer perspective, this never translates into a good experience.

Our own Chet Biggers, information systems manager, says, "It says something about the commitment of a company that has these things together and is then able to continually build on a standardized platform. Rolling out new programs is possible when your infrastructure is in place."

The good news is that the availability and costs of these new systems are now within reach even for small networks. David Gosman continues, "I think what you are seeing is that small-business owners are starting to understand and embrace these technologies. They are adopting them within their businesses in order to help them compete more effectively against larger retailers."

Bringing the Stars into Alignment

Being prepared in the right place when the right time comes along can put you in a strategic position to execute with phenomenal results. Once in a great while all the stars come into alignment and things fall into place as a result of hard work, relationship building, the foresight to know what emerging technologies are going to resonate with customers, and, of course, a little luck.

Our early desire and attempts at recognizing and rewarding those customers talking about Tasti D-Lite within social networks led us to putting a mechanism in place to do just that. This would come in the form of the first ever "social-friendly" loyalty application that featured integrations with Twitter, Facebook, and foursquare. Tying together loyalty transactions at the point of sale with social mentions was for many the holy grail of social loyalty marketing. Taking it a step further and automating location-based check-ins, as we found out, would be even better.

In the year 2009 many of the components we were building started to work together as a single engine that would support the Tasti D-Lite franchise network. Also, our investment in social technologies as well as in key relationships put us in a strong position to be able to innovate on an enterprise level.

Once we had networkwide point-of-sale systems in place, we were able to implement a loyalty program in which customers could earn and redeem points at all locations. Integrating this loyalty program with social networks seemed like a natural extension of both our POS deployments and all the social campaigns we had implemented to that point. This included something that had never been done before, which was to bring together location-based services and loyalty card swipes at the cash register. Our discussions with foursquare up to that point had revolved around check-in specials for businesses, and we started to see more customers using the application at our stores. We cover this in greater detail in Chapter 9, "The Location Business."

Having the same hardware, software, and loyalty processor across locations allowed us to implement the right solution, but it was our experience and investment in rewarding customers that allowed us to see why some additional features and benefits made complete sense. This was the kind of program one would expect from a national chain which would allow customers to earn and redeem points but with a little extra social kick. In January 2010 our social-friendly TastiRewards program was fully launched with integration to Twitter and foursquare. Soon after, the Facebook integration was completed.

Within our myTasti.com portal, users can optionally and securely connect their loyalty account to their personal Twitter, Facebook, and/or foursquare accounts. When purchases are made, messages are sent out to the users' social network as if they had posted them. In other words, the loyalty activity is shared with friends and followers when a point-of-sale transaction takes place. The foursquare tie-in allows us to effectively turn what was an active check-in on a mobile device into a passive check-in just through the swiping of a loyalty card when a purchase is made. For enabling these social postings, customers earn extra points toward free Tasti D-Lite.

This program has not only helped us reward our customers for their digital activity, but it has enabled us to create stronger connections within social channels. Making it convenient for users to share allows us to extend a message and drive awareness to their network of friends.

SNAP

Sometimes technical solutions and strategic relationships go farther than anticipated. In the case of our loyalty program, what started out as an extension of our POS vendor's software would eventually grow into a much larger platform. Because of our early involvement in the concept, an invitation was extended to us to be part of a new social loyalty solution in the form of equity in the start-up SNAP (Social Network Appreciation Platform).

This spin-off now has integrations set up with large point-of-sale vendors as well as loyalty processors and has the potential to serve thousands of merchants and millions of customers. As we write this more than two years after our TastiRewards launch, other brands are just now getting their feet wet with social loyalty through SNAP. Beyond the social posting of loyalty transactions, leaderboards and badges can be configured as part of a SNAP implementation to provide additional interactive elements for loyalty customers.

What to Look For in a Social Network

With so many channels and devices available and in use by customers these days, competing on the social plane is easier and can be more cost-effective than traditional advertising.

Many applications are actually being built with the little guy in mind. We asked foursquare's then director of business development, Tristan Walker, about how it has helped level the playing field for smaller merchants that compete with much larger brands. "The business tools on foursquare are the same for the local mom-and-pop shop as they are for the Starbucks and Walmarts of the world. We've democratized the ability to acquire new customers and to retain loyal ones. We're fans of the smaller guys. That's how we started, and we wanted to make it as simple as it is for the larger brands to engage with their customers."

Find an emerging social or mobile platform that your customers are using and get creative. Start before the early majority, and you'll be poised to not only capture market share but to benefit from some earned media exposure as well. We cover more about becoming a launch partner with a new technology in Chapter 9, "The Location Business."

Media Crossover

A cursory look at social networks like LinkedIn, Twitter, and Facebook will reveal the individual profiles of media types of all kinds. Authors, journalists, radio and television personalities, and many others are all tuning in to get the latest news and information. This is where the traditional and new media worlds are colliding since many of the conversations that are starting online make their way into more traditional media outlets. Those writing the stories have better and faster access to valuable sources. And those with something to share may find it easier to get heard.

Our online efforts over the years have landed us mentions of Tasti D-Lite in numerous offline media including the *New York Times*, *Inc. Magazine*, *Entrepreneur Magazine*, and CNBC and the cover of *Hospitality Technology* magazine. One might also expect the industry-related coverage in publications *QSR Magazine*, *PR Week*, *Advertising Age*, *Franchise Times*, and *Nation's Restaurant News*, but Tasti D-Lite has been profiled even in unrelated outlets such as *Billboard* magazine and Japan's TV Tokyo which broadcasts to millions. (More on that appearance in Chapter 9, "The Location Business.")

When it comes to public speaking, conference organizers are always looking for brands with interesting case studies and customer engagement stories. Being able to share the Tasti D-Lite story with dozens of audiences both domestically and internationally has led to many other interesting opportunities. People from many different parts of the world have heard about Tasti D-Lite and Planet Smoothie as a result of presentations like "Using Social Technologies to Reward Customers for Their Digital Activity" or "The Social Future." Headlining and key-noting at conferences and events continues to reinforce and feed the conversations and our presence online. Just asking for or submitting a "call for speakers" proposal can start opening doors very quickly. Also, volunteering to sit on a panel is a great way to meet other speakers or authors and establish a relation-ship with conference producers.

Probably one of the final destinations of online buzz is books. Books have always offered a resting place for information in the physical realm. Seven different books published in 2011 profiled Tasti D-Lite in one way or another. We include a list of these works and their authors at the end of this chapter. This is again another medium that reaches outside of online circles to perhaps touch those who would not otherwise be a part of the online conversation. Once a good story spreads around the web, it's just a matter of time before someone puts it on paper. As we chal-lenged you in Chapter 1, "Introduction to a Tasti Story," take your own journey and tell the story. Everyone loves a good story.

We've been honored over the years to receive recognition with several industry awards in categories such as breakthrough customer engagement innovation and technological achieve-ment and excellence alongside much larger companies such as Domino's Pizza, Subway, and KFC. At some level, recog-nition from industry groups has served to validate our efforts in building an effective franchise system. Being able to offer award-winning solutions to existing and prospective fran-chisees as well as to customers has an obvious benefit from a growth perspective.

Perhaps the ultimate industry and peer recognition was Jim's induction to the International Franchise Association's Hall of Fame in 2011. This highlighted the contribution he has made to the advancement of franchising and the franchising community.

Our point of this section is that leadership is a choice. When it comes to meeting the needs of customers and serving your industry, why wait for others to blaze a trail for you? That desire needs to originate from within those in a position to influence. The tools now exist for just about any business to have an influence and to begin finding new ways to reach customers.

Don't Be Invisible

So what kind of competitive advantage does high visibility online have for a franchise? The world of franchise development and lead generation has changed dramatically. People researching a franchise online will go around the traditional portals and include other social networks and channels in their search results.

We hear from many loyal customers interested in opening their own Tasti D-Lite franchise. Others hear about us from a variety of sources. Kim Falcone fields calls in our Franklin office. Kim shares, "When people are talking to other frozen dessert concepts, the competitors are bringing up Tasti D-Lite and saying how they are different and better. Many of them are naturally curious and want to know who we are, what we are doing, and why they are talking about us. All these other brands talking about Tasti D-Lite is really helping drive people to us."

Bonnie Rhinehardt, our vice president of operations, adds, "If I were a potential franchisee, that's what I would look for. How much engagement are you doing with the public and how much are you marketing your brand? If you're not marketing your brand, I'm not interested in coming on board."

The Heart of the Matter

We're thinking that you don't have time to wait around for someone else to meet the needs of your customers. The opportunity has never been greater, and neither has the responsibility. Your desire to capture the hearts of those customers has to be stronger than whatever fears or discomfort you face. Find and invest in strategic relationships with those who share your values and objectives. The tools are out there, and size doesn't matter, so get creative and do something worth talking about.

Brands are increasingly going outside of core service and product offerings and setting themselves apart by establishing value and leadership in different ways. Consumers are looking for these qualities. What good is this company doing in the world? All other things being equal, they will choose the business that is making a difference.

Books That Mention Tasti D-Lite

The Third Screen by Chuck Martin, http://www.mobilefuture institute.com/mobile1/books/the-third-screen, Nicholas Brealey Publishing, May 2011.

Social Location Marketing by Simon Salt, http://www.theinc slingers.com/the-book/, Que Publishing, February 2011.

Social Networking Made Easy by Miriam Salpeter, http://www .socialnetworkingforcareersuccess.com/, LearningExpress, May 2011.

Location-Based Marketing for Dummies by Aaron Strout and Mike Schneider (foreword by BJ Emerson), http://location basedmarketingfordummies.com/, John Wiley & Sons, Inc., September 2011.

Likeable Social Media by Dave Kerpen, http://www.likeable book.com/, McGraw-Hill, June 2011.

The Power of foursquare by Carmine Gallo, http://www.power offoursquare.com/, McGraw-Hill, September 2011.

The End of Business as Usual by Brian Solis, http://www.brian solis.com/books/, John Wiley & Sons, Inc., October 2011.

CHAPTER 8

Brand Stewardship

You must know for which harbor you
are headed, if you are to catch the
right wave to take you there.
—Seneca

W ith great opportunity comes great responsibility. Brand management in this day and age also comes with great accountability.

Ask the question "Who owns the brand?" and you'll get a wide variety of spirited responses. We asked our vice president of marketing Donna Smith the question, and she responded with, "The consumer owns the brand in the sense that the 'brand' is a perception of the product and the associated experience that exists in the customers' minds. Everything we do, from the design of the store to the uniforms to each interaction that they have had with a Tasti team member, has an impact on the perception of the brand to the consumers."

Fine-tuning that brand messaging comes through the listening we talk about in Chapter 2, "The Race for Transparency." Donna continues, "Understanding how the Tasti D-Lite and Planet Smoothie brands are differentiated from others in the minds of the consumers lets us know how we are doing with the messaging and the customer experience that we are delivering to them."

From a legal and contractual perspective, clearly the trademark holder has a vested interest in and responsibility for protecting and defending the brand name. So what level of trust and control is appropriate for the consumers of a product or service? And what happens if the image and culture has already been established around a product, as in our case? Rick Cornish served as our interim chief marketing officer in the early days just after the acquisition of Tasti D-Lite in 2007. To the latter question he says, "This situation was unique: In the absence of any marketing communications in the first 20 years of Tasti's existence, it was the consumer who was in control of the marketing conversation. By aligning our initial efforts with that established passion for the Tasti D-Lite brand, we multiplied the effect of what we were doing—fueling their enthusiasm while bridging their connection from the old Tasti to the new."

As a nontraditional area developer, Scott Hughes opens Tasti D-Lite and Planet Smoothie locations in places like college campuses, within airports, and inside Walmart stores. He says, "It's more important than ever for brands to know what they stand for, what principles they believe in, know what they can't change, and know what they can change. You can't trust your customers with the brand unless you're confident and comfortable with who your brand is. All great companies trust customers with the brand."

For this conversation, we need to start with what or who goes into building a brand. Among other things, this requires both creators and curators. Understanding the fundamental differences in each will go a long way toward developing culture and ultimately brand stewardship.

Creators

We are all consumers. We are not all creators. Perhaps more accurately, we do not all demonstrate the creative traits that we possess as much as we could. Whether or not you subscribe to that concept, the creative energies we all pour into our work can be clearly seen.

In many ways, entrepreneurs are creators. They invent new processes and products, build and expand, merge and multiply. They can't help it. Whether it's creating a great customer service experience or developing a new business model, they have the attributes needed to accomplish great things.

As director of franchise services for Tasti D-Lite, Dedria (or Dee as we call her) periodically attends openings of new Tasti D-Lite and Planet Smoothie locations around the country. She uses her creative and brilliant photography skills to capture the emotion and the visible sense of accomplishment involved with a franchise opening. She offers, "To be able to open a store is not an easy process. I find great satisfaction in capturing this extraordinary moment for the owners. Having friends and family come to witness the opening of a new business is huge, and I feel being able to provide them with professional photos of all the hugs, happiness, and activity is important. I care that when they walk away from the process they feel proud and cared about. I know it sounds cheesy, but I want people to feel loved."

Dee captured this touching photo at the opening of Tasti D-Lite in Franklin, Tennessee, unaware that the subjects were the father (Eddie) and nephew (Max) of the new owner Kent Patterson.

Captured: Some Tasti with Granddad

You can tell who the creators are from the consumers. The creators are the ones who stand out from the crowd and make things happen. Dee takes it a step further and adds, "You can't fake caring about what you are doing and where you work. You have to attach yourself to something more than your paycheck, whether that is the people or to a piece of the brand."

We could not agree more. In our opinion, going to work every day just for a paycheck is the height of poverty thinking.

Chapter 3, "Going Behind the Brand," touches on content creators and digital natives. Blending these individuals with those who have the business acumen and experience in managing relationships is critical. Media is in the DNA of those now entering the workforce, and even older companies are starting to understand the value of people who are comfortable with creating content online.

Director of franchise services Steve Rothenstein is a key player in helping scale the Tasti D-Lite culture globally. When he started in late 2007, he was part of the transition and conversion that occurred at the corporate level in New York City, and he eventually moved to Tennessee. He offers, "There are some people that have a hard time operating within an entrepreneurial company. This requires free thought and not waiting for instructions that may not come. You cannot be solely a consumer. You need to have at least one of those other traits in you in order to be indispensable in a company attempting to do what we are trying to do."

Curators

We are creators by nature, but curators by choice. What does this have to do with brand building? Where you have great stories and examples of vocal and passionate brand advocates, curating this information becomes just as much of an opportunity as creation of new content. Pushing out regular updates and educating consumers about the benefits of a product or service is a fundamental part of an effective content strategy, but with all the unsolicited comments, praise, and criticism flowing through the web, there's a different kind of corporate responsibility at play. Stewarding these valuable data becomes a big part of the brand manager's job description. This curated content will serve the organization in a number of ways:

1. These stories become part of the brand and its identity. Thomas Scott introduced the brand journalism concept to us in Chapter 5.
2. We can now push these insights and customer perspectives into the rest of the organization.
3. The data collected allow us to make better marketing decisions and serve the needs of our customers more effectively.

Curation involves listening, collecting, and organizing, but it goes beyond just stories. Images and other digital media also become important brand assets.

We started installing "TastiPads" in new locations in early 2011. Among the various functions of these iPad-based customer kiosks is a simple guestbook application that allows customers to let us know about their visit. While the concept is no different from the old-school guest book that customers can sign, a hosted, database-powered version has obvious benefits.

Comments like, "Tasti rocks! Glad it finally got here!" and "I had a complicated order, and y'all really accommodated me." may not seem like much taken individually, but trends in customer service become evident over time.

What's better than a customer testimonial? Well, a *Tasti*monial of course. These customer quotes can be found on franchisee web pages and give Tasti D-Lite owners a way to capture local feedback and share the fun with others online. Each of these examples has different levels of moderation.

For years, letters, calls, and then e-mails came in from customers wanting to share their love for Tasti. Being a good brand steward means capturing and archiving this great content. We found tales of marriage proposals in Tasti D-Lite locations, celebrity sightings (including one who will remain unnamed who appeared to enjoy not only one or two, but four samples and then simply walked out), pets who love Tasti as well as more entertaining comments like, "If Tasti D-Lite frozen yogurt were a woman, it would have a restraining order against me."[1]

Beyond what we found online, our research for this book included discussions with many Tasti D-Lite franchisees and a visit to the archive of e-mails from years past.

There's the couple who got engaged at a Tasti D-Lite location after studying there together for many months. We were able to help them celebrate by providing treats at their wedding reception.

This e-mail came in from a sibling named Jessica, "My sister is OBSESSED with Tasti D-Lite everytime we come to NYC before we even get on the plane—ACTUALLY the minute the plane tickets are booked to be exact—she won't shut up about her favorite fro-yo! Now as fate has it she is moving to NYC (no not because of the tasti-d-lite but I have no doubt it was high on the 'pro' list!) and I would love nothing more than to wish her Bon voyage with a fabulous pack of never-ending tasti-d-lite gift certificates. Now the question—do you carry them? If so, how do I purchase???!!!! Thanks a ton! :-)"

In south Florida, there have been requests by children and parents to know the exact color of our Tasti pink brand wall. Apparently there are now several bedrooms painted in this color.

This rather desperate e-mail came in from Anna, "This is more than a general inquiry—this is desperation talking!!! PLEASE PLEASE PLEASE open your stores here in Michigan. I was fortunate enough to come across one while in Florida—Michigan is so damn behind on all the really cool things. So PLEASE open a bunch here. I know they would be a HUGE hit. I just can't get in my car to drive to NY or FLA to get my fix. So PLEASE!!!"

Founder Celeste Carlesimo has heard quite a few stories over the years. "I remember when we only had stores in Manhattan, how the chauffeurs would drive their clients into the city to stock up on Tasti. I even had customers who bought machines for their homes and bought gallons from me so they could enjoy Tasti 24/7. If I was in the store and someone found out who I was, I would be swamped by them all praising me for creating Tasti D-Lite and our wonderful flavors. I remember when Al Roker stood in line with other customers while he was losing his weight. I remember reporters who swore that we added something addictive to our product because they could not believe the loyalty we inspired from our customers and the way they came every day to our stores. Our customers mapped out their day according to their Tasti stops. Most of all the many boyfriends and husbands who were sent out to stand in line and call their significant others with a list of the day's flavors, so they could bring them home a little bit of heaven."

With all the customer stories that we would hear, we needed a way to gather more testimonials of those who have benefited by making Tasti a part of a healthier lifestyle. Our Tasti Healthy

Habit Search was born to capture these experiences and to recognize and reward those who shared them. Hundreds of entries
came in when the program was launched in April 2011. Each
month a winner was identified, interviewed, professionally pho-
tographed, and profiled on our microsite tastihabit.com. One
thousand dollars and a month of free Tasti D-Lite were awarded
to people like Jennifer Wiley. She fell in love with Tasti D-Lite
and ate it for lunch daily when she lived in New York City but
was separated until a new location opened in her neighborhood
in Maryland. In her words: "When it came to my area, I started
having Tasti D-Lite for dessert almost every day. After dinner,
I would go to the gym. And after the gym, I would have Tasti
D-Lite. I would say to myself, 'If you want to do the gym, and
you do well, here's a snack you can have.' With all my other
habits, Tasti gave me extra motivation to get through my day."

Jay Justilian found Tasti D-Lite in a much different way
when he heard about a weight loss contest being held at our
Houston franchise location. He made Tasti D-Lite a part of his
overall diet plan and lost 48 pounds.

Winner Heather Graboyes is on a first name basis with South
Florida area developer Robyn Vescovi. In Heather's words,
"Having something refreshing and nutritious is what has kept
me going. Every day, I get a 'flavor of the day' alert for both of
the centers, or as I call it, 'Tasti Time.' It helps me know which
store I want to go to that day. It's one of the highlights of my day."

Joeleen Tepper's story had to do with the birth of her baby:
"I've always been a Tasti D fan (for at least 15 years). During my
pregnancy, I had trouble keeping down a lot of foods. I found
out I could eat Tasti, though, so I was there all the time. Tasti
helped me get through it. Best of all, with help from Tasti, I'm
back down to my pre-baby weight after six months. Hooray! I
lost approximately 30 to 35 pounds after my pregnancy."

Molly McCarthy was a winner in late 2011 and got a special surprise when she watched one of the *30 Rock* episodes on
TV with her family and they saw her pictures on posters in the
windows of the Tasti D-Lite location in Manhattan's Columbus
Circle where the taping took place.

The Wall of Happiness

Beyond simple feedback, which can be quite mechanical from a process standpoint, it is the responsibility of those on the social front lines to help impart the customer perspective to the rest of the organization. But with all the great technology available to help provide visibility to customer insights, it is tempting to overthink how simple it can be to communicate these insights internally, to our franchisees, and even within Tasti D-Lite locations. Enter our "wall of happiness."

Our mission is published as follows: "Making every customer's day better by serving great tasting products as a celebration of life, health, and happiness." Providing a visual along these lines came in the form of an inspiration from another brand whose employees keep track of customer comments on a "wall of awesome."

Our growing repository of joy at our Franklin, Tennessee, home office consists of a simple but large bulletin board that has postcard-sized printouts of unsolicited quotes and references to Tasti D-Lite. From all over the globe customers broadcast their Tasti experiences to friends or followers on social channels of all kinds.

Low tech: The wall of happiness brings the virtual conversation into the physical space.

Curation Platforms

Bringing together consumers and the products they love requires going beyond bulletin boards. From the low tech we move on to one of the more recent applications that has quickly risen in popularity. Pinterest allows users to collect, share, and comment on images across the web. Items of interest are "pinned" to a users "board" and are usually linked to the source of the photo, video, or discussion. Here, the trifecta of consumption, creation, and curation is obvious.

As marketing coordinator of social and digital platforms, Katherine Gosney looks at new social tools to see what opportunities they present for Tasti D-Lite and Planet Smoothie. We asked Katherine why this social site had gotten so popular. "Facebook and Twitter are great channels for people to use to speak their minds. It's all about status updates and what they think is cool or not cool. A site like Pinterest allows people to share things that they find to be beautiful, exciting, or amusing through pictures. I believe it allows people to take a break from all the chatter and explore and speak with a different part of their mind that is sometimes unable to be expressed through Facebook."

Here, brands are also participating and sharing other people's ideas and photos. The follower mechanism is still in place, but it's more than subscribing to a single feed. Different boards within a single account allow others to decide what is relevant based on their interests. Katherine continues, "Since you have different boards, people can choose which ones they wish to follow. For instance, our Tasti D-Lite account has a New York City board, so a New Yorker may choose to follow that one but not the Tennessee or Arizona boards. Users have the power to choose."

People and businesses are quickly starting to see that Pinterest is driving traffic to their blogs, websites, or other online resources. Being able to capture and archive content about Tasti D-Lite via Pinterest allows us to manage and share what we see as valuable brand assets.

The Cycle of Transparency

Cultivating and communicating core values and vision on a regular basis have become part of the ethos of many great businesses. Periodically, we have all-staff meetings at the home office; these are called Eagle Renewal meetings. In these important gatherings we recalibrate, let our hair down a little, and hear presentations from different departments to help us understand in more detail what everyone does within the company. These meetings typically include the latest findings from around the web so we can see what customers have been up to. Making this a priority has, we think, made a difference culturally because the insights we share and the resulting emotional connections make their way around the office.

Why is all this important? What does it do for our corporate culture? How does it impact the decisions we make every day? The more we can impart concepts and insights internally, the more they are going to influence what we do. The resulting choices made at the home office around operations, marketing, and technology make their way into our franchise network and eventually back to the customer. This cycle of transparency only continues to grow and gain as much momentum as we allow.

It's the Culture, Stupid (as Told by BJ)

I am regularly invited to talk about our journey from social negligence to becoming a social-friendly brand. After one conference session, a member of the audience asked, "Why Tasti D-Lite? I mean what is it about your company that put you in this position to be a leader in this space? Does it have something to do with your culture?"

My answer at the time was not as articulate (or as accurate) as it could have been, so I'll take the opportunity now to try to redeem myself here.

I believe that any social presence will ultimately be the digital manifestation and reflection of a corporate culture. While that organization's mission, vision, and values should be reflected in its online presence, people should be able to see a culture that empowers the associates within it—empowered to make decisions that touch customers.

You have to have champions in the C-suite. An effective online presence won't happen otherwise because the resources won't get allocated to social media.

Policies and guidelines provide the framework and structure for the activities and content as they should in any organization, but culture determines the spirit. Culture will determine the depth of authentic interaction and often the results. Policies are generally defensive in nature and exist to protect things like trademarks. Culture helps determine the offensive posture. Policies protect, but real results are determined by culture and the values that drive it.

Cultural Autonomy

On corporate culture, Steve Rothenstein says, "You can't purposefully create it but you easily can kill it. You can't force people to be happy when they are not. So it has to come naturally through the people that you hire. Then you have to allow the people to be who they are. Management needs to allow it and embrace it even if they don't like all the things that are happening within the culture as it develops."

Good intentions can still kill a culture. The environment has to be allowed to exist, and you have to have the vision to see it and then the patience and courage to support it over the long haul. The fundamental value is trust. Values like trust, accountability, and respect are empowering in that they inform us of what to do and what not to do. These are the standards that determine and detect priorities.

As an extension of this concept, even private equity and venture capital firms that once relished anonymity today find themselves being out front in support of brand transparency. Here we have to pause and give credit to our own financial partners at Snow Phipps Group for their willingness to allow Tasti D-Lite and now Planet Smoothie to have the autonomy to expand social efforts as needed.

If you are looking for a source of capital to expand your business and grow, you are going to want investors who understand the value of building a brand the way we've been talking about.

Hiring for Transparency

What is traditionally called human resources we call *people services*. Every member of the organization must come through the matrix of values clearly outlined in the job description and interview process. While people services are the gateway to the business, job candidates must determine whether they agree with those core values and qualify or disqualify themselves accordingly.

The values we have established over the last several years are trust, accountability, integrity, caring, respect, dignity, and enthusiasm. Together with our mission and vision statements, they provide not only a filter as we grow, but they also help guide us in our daily decision making and interactions with others both inside and outside the company.

Establishing and reviewing these values and statements have become a standard part of our AOP (annual operating planning) meetings. Here, everyone has an opportunity to weigh in on what is important in order to build a brand and culture that will last. Considering the time and energy we put in at our place of employment, we have to be intentional about where we are going and how we are going to get there.

Transparency and Customer Service

Regarding the new digital natives coming into the workforce, it will be interesting to see what kind of skills will translate well into things like customer service. If they have an appreciation for transparency as consumers, will they act different when they are on the other side of the transaction? Just because they are more social-friendly, we can't assume that the next generation of digital natives will be more customer-friendly. We would like to think, however, that there should be some implication and correlation between these things. They may understand that marketing is no longer a one-way message, but what will their conversation look like? We can see a linear relationship between transparent, consumer-friendly service and profit. One would hope that the distance between the head and the heart for those now entering the workforce will be shorter.

It's been said that you are only as good as your weakest link in customer service. Fostering loyalty means putting the right people in the right seats on the bus.

Brand Attitude

We were fascinated by the customer-operator dynamic that existed in the original New York City locations for many years. There seemed to be a mutual understanding and expectation between Tasti D-Lite customers and the operators of the licensed outlets that served the product. At the time we had limited product offerings with only select flavors available "on tap" on any given day. Customers would glance in the window to see what flavors were on tap and either settle for what was being offered or perhaps walk a few blocks to see what other locations had available. The joke became that with over 100 flavors, finding your favorite on any given day was akin to winning the lottery as Sam D, who we introduced in Chapter 1, explains: "Nothing beats the feeling you get when you walk into a 'Tasti D,' impulsively looking to the back to discover the two flavors of the day, and one of them just perfectly fits your mood/ This lottery feature makes eating frozen dessert not only delicious, but surprising and nerve-racking!"

As interesting as this emotional dynamic sounds, customer expectations at the point of sale remained relatively low, and the majority of the operators simply accommodated them by quickly dispensing the product to keep the lines moving. There was little need for the formalities or discussion that might be required for a transaction having more options. At the time, this met the basic needs of the customer, which was to get their Tasti and be on their way. No frills, just a consistent product served quickly, which was somewhat reminiscent of the "soup man" episodes from the popular *Seinfeld* TV show that captured this attitude in New York so well during the period.

One blogger recalls her Tasti D-Lite experience of the mid-1990s this way: "Buying Tasti-D-Lite was not an entirely pleasant experience. Most of the stores were poorly lit holes in the wall, and the line to order often snaked out the door and down the street. The women who worked there were unfriendly and unhelpful more often than not. And yet I kept going back for small servings of french vanilla, angel food cake, rice pudding, apple pie, coconut, cake batter, and strawberry colada—all smothered in rainbow sprinkles and/or granola (which was a perfect complement to apple pie)."[2]

Over time, this arrangement became part of the experience and culture of Tasti D-Lite, but sustainability would become an issue as the economic and competitive landscape changed. New customers finding Tasti in other markets had both options and questions. A greater level of customer service was not optional even in the legacy units.

The online presence during this period was consistent with the offline attitude. The original website made available only the necessary information and offered little along the lines of interaction or brand experience. Perhaps this met customer needs initially, but the shift toward brand transparency was beginning, and this change was certain to affect even the most popular of concepts everywhere.

The new franchise model was equipped to meet a different expectation as well as to offer a fuller customer experience. As more line extensions and product offerings were developed, the dynamic changed and the need for education and discussion became a reality and an opportunity for more engagement. Keeping the surprise and delight factors intact while providing more options like the any-flavor-at-any-time custom-blended treats became a priority. The familiar flavor boards remained for those wanting a little adventure. Otherwise a favorite could be prepared on demand. Throw in a self-serve model, and the dynamic shifts again.

Creating an online presence from scratch for a brand that had earned a reputation that identified with the sassy market that conceived it was an interesting venture. Injecting a little New York attitude into the social network feeds without being rude actually seemed to augment the brand voice online and bring a little fun to the conversation. So the question became how much of a reflection of the regional culture do you put into the online content? With most of the interaction taking place with those within New York, it almost felt as if it was expected, and this allowed us to capitalize on the history of the brand within this new application of technology. Pushing that envelope would prove to be a trial-and-error process, but overall it gave us some freedom to experiment more than we would have had otherwise.

However, the New York flavor of the brand voice would not seem appropriate to those discovering Tasti in new markets. As we opened new locations in the south and west, the voice that met these new customers would need to be adjusted given that the Tasti experience had to be more in line with regional customs, such as Southern hospitality.

Empowering franchisees to manage the localized feeds on sites like Facebook and Twitter allows us to provide something we could not accomplish otherwise. Their knowledge of the local scene and the types of customers they are catering to within their area better meets the needs of the community online and off.

Within the image or culture of the brand there needs to be continuity, but the cultural dialect may need to be tuned to meet the needs of each market. As we discuss in Chapter 2, "The Race for Transparency," the franchise model fits well here.

Dual-Brand Dynamics

If managing one brand presence online was not interesting enough, adding another brand in late 2011 would bring a new dynamic and opportunity to engage a whole new fanatical community. Having Planet Smoothie come along as a sister brand to Tasti D-Lite would raise some significant questions. How would the two brands interact and support each other online? Would they relate like siblings and poke fun at each other? With two sets of customers craving products in complementary categories, the cross-promotional potential for both concepts was huge.

Developing unique and independent but aligned personalities specifically to interact online and reflect the culture of each brand is not something many others had done to this point. Success in this area would start with knowing the facets and qualities of each customer base enough to reflect an accurate brand persona that would resonate effectively. Above all, we really just wanted to have some fun. With Smoothie names like Chocolate Elvis, 2 Piece Bikini, and Shag-a-delic, who wouldn't?

Our first campaign came in the form of a cosponsorship and giveaway for the Channing Tatum and Rachel McAdams movie *The Vow*. Having both brands cross-promote and participate in the giveaway allowed us to break the ice and help introduce the brand relationship.

In 2012, the first cobranded Tasti D-Lite and Planet Smoothie locations celebrated their grand openings. This allowed us to introduce the brand mascot characters and create some fun content for the web as they interacted at the events. More on these characters in Chapter 10, "Meet Your Cocreators."

Be Responsible

Being a part of a community means being responsible with the content that is created. The first version of our TastiRewards social integration, which we first discuss in Chapter 7, "Rolling with the Big Boys," had one standard message that members could send to friends and followers saying, "I just earned (X) TastiRewards points at Tasti D-Lite [location]." These posts would automatically appear when a loyalty card was used during a purchase. The TastiRewards program received great press, blog posts, and articles about the initial features. Now we really needed to address the fact that seeing these posts could get old fairly quickly depending upon how often TastiRewards members frequented Tasti D-Lite.

In short order, we modified our application so that users could choose between a dozen or more different messages, some of which were actually provided by customers. The system would randomize the posts that were preauthorized, and we added the ability to include links to coupons so that friends could benefit as well from the loyalty activity of others.

Azdmelani
@azdmelani

WooHoo! Im racking up the TastiRewards points over here at Tasti D-Lite 3rd Ave and 92nd St NYC. http://myTasti.com/

TastiRewards message: A preauthorized creative myTasti.com post triggered by the use of a loyalty card.

It would be in no one's best long-term interest to clutter up communities with spamlike content. Designing responsible social media marketing campaigns is a part of good brand stewardship. From a culture standpoint, operating in the spirit of the community requires not only creative thinking but the right approach from the brand. Ultimately how each business either creates value or takes away from a given community will speak volumes, and the business will yield the fruit that its efforts deserve.

A Day at Tasti

One of the programs that we developed is called "A Day at Tasti." Here, our home office associates have a chance to spend a day in a store and get a really good understanding of the products, equipment, and technology that touch the public. Actually participating in making products, interacting with customers, and answering questions can have a great impact when it comes to making decisions back at the office.

Our general counsel Grayson Brown was interested in seeing the response of customers when he told them who he was: "The response from customers was remarkable. They loved to hear that executives were working behind the counter to get more experience with customers and the product. Getting out from behind the desk and engaging customers face-to-face says that we are invested in the customer relationship. We desire to know what is on their minds so that we can create a better tomorrow for them at Tasti."

Supply chain manager Gary Foltynewicz had never worked in retail. He admits to having shipped railcars of goods to Kenya, but until his Day at Tasti, he had never handed a product to a customer over the counter. "I saw the frontline perspective of what it takes to sell a cup of our product. I want to try to do it periodically because it makes what I do here real and tangible."

Stewarding the Negative

Human nature dictates that critical reviews and condemning comments that threaten the brand should be hidden and avoided at all costs. Mechanisms such as the "like" or "retweet" buttons empower users with the ability to praise or vilify a brand at the touch of a button, and the content lasts forever. Control is not an option, and the more relevant and popular the subject matter is, the stickier it is going to be with search engines. The approach business owners take in such matters ultimately speaks volumes about how secure they feel with their product and themselves.

More and more consumers are turning to online networks as their preferred customer service line for expressing frustrations. The telephone is not as convenient for them to communicate a concern, and they would rather do it in the online world they are accustomed to. Easy for them, but a concern for businesses now faced with the challenge of monitoring and managing the content and conversations on multiple channels.

Everyone loves praise. We love it when customers share positive experiences through word of mouth. There may be ways however that can make criticism more valuable than praise.

Negative reviews can provide the following:

1. They force a business to listen more effectively. Smart companies use the tools available to understand what is going on in the virtual realm. The faster they can listen, the faster they can correct misinformation and provide the corporate perspective.
2. They force change within the organization. Addressing criticism and bad reviews frequently brings a healthy dose of reality to the corporate office. The perspective that this information can provide is often an eye-opener for many people who sit behind desks all day. Customers are closer than ever, and a few mouse clicks can provide more information than the focus groups and surveys of yesterday.
3. They provide an opportunity for the company to provide some over-the-top service and turn a disgruntled customer into a brand advocate.

Our friend Jack Monson says, "There's always the possibility of receiving comments that can be damaging. At some point every brand and company is going to get complaints and criticism. So much so that suspicions arise when there is nothing but positive comments for a given business. It's possible but unlikely. On Facebook business pages, for example, posts created by consumers can be moderated by the administrators. Posts can be deleted at any time. Leaving those complaints

intact demonstrates that the business is serious about solving problems."

Jack continues, "Consider the airline industry where there is a proliferation of consumer frustrations voiced online. These are many times not addressed due in part to the sheer volume of complaints. So when you have an airline that does take the initiative to at least listen, respond, and try to answer the tough questions, the consumer sentiment is going to be greater for that company. There is going to be a better feeling about that brand because they are stepping up and are publicly addressing issues. It's easy to say the problem is just too big and not take a step toward a solution."

Here are some additional thoughts on dealing with negative comments:

1. The fact that you are responding is part of winning the battle. Negative comments that are left untouched without response look twice as bad. Showing that you actually care is a big part of being a responsible business online.
2. Respond where the issue originated. A canned response in a broad release from the president of the company is not what the community is hoping for. It wants to see a personalized effort to respond where the concern was raised.
3. If you've invested in relationships, created a culture, and built your brand well enough, one comment here or there is going to be discredited. Any potentially damaging information gathered from the various online channels will put organizations in a position to:
   a. Try to bury undesirable content with better content, praying that the search engines will be kind.
   b. Put their head in the sand and pretend it does not exist.
   c. Embrace reality and make a change.

Smart companies are embracing reality, making the hard decisions, and building better products and pursuing better service. If you don't like reality, change it. Steward your brand by listening and making better products and services.

The Heart of the Matter

Effective stewardship and brand building has everything to do with effective people and culture building. Shared core values, a strong ethical base, a positive belief in people, and compelling vision are all vital for sustainability in today's organizations.

We all consume, but to create is to give. When we share life through words, actions, images, feelings, and experiences we find fulfillment and pleasure. Building a brand means collecting these experiences and using them to fuel future experiences.

As individuals, we have to be a culture of one before we can contribute or be an asset within another culture. Being out of touch and unable to participate in a community can take place on an individual and a corporate level. Healthy people and brands decide who they are, what they want to be, and where they are going.

CHAPTER 9

The Location Business

> It is easy to dodge our responsibilities,
> but we cannot dodge the consequences
> of dodging our responsibilities.
> —*Sir Josiah Stamp*

The new dimension that location-based mobile applications have opened has made a significant impact on the humanization of businesses. Accountability at the local level will continue to be something that brick-and-mortar business owners deal with on multiple fronts, as mobile applications and social networks allow customers to provide reviews and share their experiences with others on a more granular level. Greater access to information coupled with the ability to share detail related to time and place is both empowering for customers and revealing for businesses.

One example might be the digitally enabled customer who walks onto the new car lot of a dealership armed with a smartphone. Information related to every detail and line item on the sticker is available to the customer, and the salesperson is faced with either being transparent with those details or losing the sale. The volumes of information and comparison data now instantly accessible can be the salesperson's best friend or dreaded foe.

Numerous applications now allow users to "check-in" or otherwise geotag their activity and share their location with friends in real time. Privacy controls allow users to share this activity with only those they choose or they can make it public. Gaming elements allow customers to compete for things like mayorships, for example, which are awarded to those who have visited a location the most often. Brands are already joining the fun with special offers and promotions for those customers who use these services. Opportunities abound for integrating conventional systems and campaigns with the experiences consumers are having on these new mobile and social applications.

The "where" dimension has come of age. Reaching consumers based on their proximity to a business has become a reality and many local merchants are already reaping great benefits. Raising awareness, attracting and retaining customers, as well as rewarding them for their loyalty are within reach for businesses that understand the value.

Now several years old, the growing popularity of applications in which physical places and venues are core objects on the network have already started to impact business as we know it.

The full implications for sales, customer service, loyalty, point of sale, and many other facets of business are still unfolding with each new application that brings the location ingredient into the mix.

Meanwhile, the integration of location into much larger platforms has helped to drive awareness and adoption of these new applications and services. The content and interaction around Google+ Local business pages (formerly Google Place pages) for example are a big part of local search engine results. Within Facebook, tagging a location or business when using a mobile device is as simple as tagging a friend or adding a photo. We talk more about the future of location and geotagging in Chapter 11, "The Social Future."

The Privacy Value Exchange

Perhaps you are wondering why people would voluntarily share their whereabouts with people they don't know. Clearly there are security and privacy concerns to be considered when dealing with mobile technology and the Internet. Sharing what is on your mind is one thing. Sharing what is on your mind at any given moment along with your exact location is entirely different. The generational differences we discuss earlier have much to do with this mindset. The shift toward this kind of transparent communication is happening, but the motivation for sharing may vary. Where is the threshold?

Asif Khan is the founder and president of the Location Based Marketing Association. He says, "If the value exchange threshold is met, users are becoming more comfortable with sharing their data. Value for some may be in the ability to see and connect with someone who might be in the area. For others, unlocking a special offer in exchange for sharing those whereabouts might be enough." What does this mean for businesses and merchants wanting to reach users on these networks? It simply means they are going to need to understand where that threshold is for their target customer and engage on the customer's terms.

In the example below, a foursquare check-in that would normally be shared with trusted friends was optionally sent to Twitter, which made it public.

BJ Emerson
@BJ_Emerson

I'm at Tasti D-lite HQ (341 Cool Springs Blvd Suite 100, Franklin) 4sq.com/yS3AFT

Public Tweet: Sample foursquare check-in automatically pushed to Twitter.

Checking into Businesses

The headway we had made with mobile couponing on Twitter in early 2009 got the attention of some Stanford Business School students who were helping develop the Business 101 case studies for the Twitter website. Shortly after these were published, one of the students contacted us to discuss a new venture called foursquare, a location-based mobile application. Not yet employed by foursquare, Tristan Walker was eager to get us on the phone with one of the cofounders of foursquare, Dennis Crowley, to explore how Tasti D-Lite and other businesses could work with foursquare to reach more customers around our locations in New York City. The application was growing in popularity in New York City, and we were already seeing that customers were starting to use the service and interact around Tasti D-Lite locations.

About that early phone call we asked Tristan, "Why Tasti?" He said, "We saw two things. From what you were doing on Twitter, we knew you were forward looking enough and second, because you guys chose us and allowed us to understand your needs and goals."

The conversation we had with Crowley led to an invitation to become launch partners for what would become foursquare's check-in specials. Initially, businesses could promote an offer that would reach potential customers within a certain distance of the physical location. When users look at nearby businesses on foursquare with their mobile device, those locations with a check-in special are highlighted on the list. All users would need to do is check in on the app which would unlock the offer. The users would then simply show their mobile device to a cashier to receive a discount or whatever the offer was.

For years we've had access to impressions and clicks, but this additional piece of key information unlocks a new dimension of opportunities. Being able to see actual check-in data was revolutionary at the time because it represented the confirmation of an actual foot-in-the-door visit to a physical location. You could then compare that with the redemptions recorded at the cash register.

We also found that foursquare was allowing us to reach outside our typical demographic given that the early adopters were primarily men. Again, the shift toward this kind of communication would eventually even out the gender demographic as more people are becoming comfortable with their privacy settings. Closing the gap between the personal mobile device and the physical retail experience was quickly becoming a reality through these types of location-based services.

This functionality would soon be extended to include "swarm" specials, "mayor" specials, and several other types of offers that would encourage customer behavior in one way or another. Getting your friends to check in at the same time as you could unlock a certain offer for all if the venue owner wanted to configure the special that way.

As of March 2012, there were some 750,000 merchants using foursquare to reach and reward consumers. While the primary impact and opportunity is for local brick-and-mortar businesses, others that are not can still interact around physical locations within foursquare. The History Channel, for example, has a brand page that can be followed. Here the value is in the "tips" that the History Channel leaves around different locations as well as other ways it interacts with users.

At this point, much of the initial publicity about this and other early location-based applications has waned, but relevance for businesses should depend upon customer adoption and not the amount of buzz or press any particular service is receiving.

Take it or leave it, the opportunity exists for businesses to be involved. What can't be ignored is the user-generated content that comes along for the location ride.

Interesting things start to happen when some online status or activity is tied to an in-store experience.

The Impact on Customer Service

As users interact around these venues, other content is created and shared along with the location data through things like tips, reviews, and ratings. This user-generated content has now gone mobile, and every element of a local business has the potential to be shared virally through the ubiquitous smartphone. Attaching details of their experience at a business has customers uncovering all kinds of surprises, both good and bad—secret items that are not listed on the menu, for instance, or what the best seat in the house is. Customer service experiences are a popular topic within these networks. Many people will report how great or helpful someone was or, perhaps more likely, wasn't. While many consumers are reluctant to complain or perhaps compliment face-to-face, inhibitions are less apparent when it comes to leaving feedback online.

Billy Ryan is general manager of our Nashville, Tennessee, location. We asked him what the impact of social and mobile technologies has been on customer service and the in-store experience. He said, "What it does is provide an avalanche of the desire to achieve excellence—from customer service, a delicious product, and immaculately clean centers."

Again, if businesses understand the big picture of what is taking place, accountability will be an issue that will need to be addressed if they have any interest in customer satisfaction. To be fair, the retail environment can be chaotic and the priority is meeting the needs of the customer in front of you. Worrying about what may or may not be happening in some virtual realm usually takes a backseat. Out of sight, out of mind, as they say. Conversely, someone who is dedicated to listening online but who is separated from the front line has the other perspective. All the while, customers are caught in the middle, but as more are interacting in the social and mobile realms, the opportunities to meet them there will increase.

Providing a seamless and consistent experience for that online and offline customer then becomes the challenge. So what happens if there is a great chasm between the online brand experience and the local retail experience? Does it do any good to provide phenomenal support in the virtual realm if the in-store experience is subpar? Our superstar director of franchise services Steve Rothenstein offers this: "Customers expect the online experience to mirror the physical. If they love our online customer service, they shouldn't go into a store and get ill-treated by the cashier or owner. It's one thing to disappoint a customer, but it's another to piss them off. That lack of continuity to me is actually worse than not having an online presence at all."

It would seem that this new challenge is related to its older cousin referred to as the "last mile" in retail. This refers to the execution of corporate initiatives at the local level. Decisions that are made at the corporate office and what actually happens in a retail store can be miles apart.

Both are threats to meeting the real needs of consumers. Part of the problem is that customers are likely dealing with different people online and in the store. Consistency at every level is critical, and while the online presence could never replace the in-store experience, it could certainly augment it in many ways. Here are a few, some of which we have touched on in other chapters:

1. **Support prior to purchase.** With more consumers doing research online, being there as a resource is important for what happens before the in-store transaction.
2. **Another set of ears.** Customers will share things online that they will not in person.

3. **After-purchase validation and support.** Questions can be fielded to support the purchase.
4. **Extending the conversation.** When the word of mouth is spread online, there are opportunities to keep the conversation going so others can participate as well.

Expectations

In light of all this, what do customers really expect? As we mention previously, consumers are interacting within these new social and mobile applications much faster than local businesses can implement any kind of process or policies around them.

We've found that many early adopters are fairly tolerant and will go out of their way to help educate the business owner on the opportunity, perhaps because they care and want to see the business take part as well. As early adopters are exploring these new applications, they want to share what they discover and what they learn is possible with technology.

It is likely, however, that they will become less tolerant over time as these technologies mature and become mainstream. The reverse of this is when a business owner gets there first and is able to meet users when they are ready. To us, this sounds like another element to, and advantage in, the race for transparency we mention in Chapter 2.

Mechanics Versus Dynamics

We came across a story of one faithful Tasti D-Lite customer who loved foursquare and also loved being mayor at the places she frequented. This designation or award is bestowed upon those who check in the most at a given venue. Other customers can always oust the foursquare mayor based on the frequency of visits. In an e-mail, Briana Severson shared this with us: "The day that I became the Mayor, I was standing in line, checking-in [on foursquare] to receive the $1 off coupon. I saw that I had become Mayor and so I excitedly told the cashier as I did a little dance. 'What does that mean?' the cashier said, seeming amused by my excitement. I replied, 'It means I come here more than anyone else. It means I'm your most loyal customer basically.'"

Do you see the missed opportunity here? While her expectations were met around the mechanics of the offer (the check-in special was honored), our inability to capture the moment prevented us from taking the experience to the next level. The larger opportunity lies within our ability to understand the dynamics and emotions that exist within these social networks and recognize and celebrate our customers.

What is happening in the very personal mobile dimension needs to be supported by the retail experience. Imagine the delight the customer could have felt if we met her in the middle instead of taking the air out of the experience. From the perspective of fostering loyalty, what is more sticky than reinforcing and supporting positive emotions?

As it turned out, we had recently been approached by the producers of a Japanese television station who were profiling businesses that used foursquare. We were looking for some customers in New York to be interviewed for a segment to be aired on TV Tokyo, so we invited Briana to be a part of the taping at our Columbus Circle location.

Briana on TV: Take the time to acknowledge and celebrate with customers.

We need to take the time to acknowledge and appreciate customers who are making the effort to check in, share their brand experience with friends, and engage with us online. "What does that mean?" Well, it means a lot to this customer, and we'd like to extend a special thanks and congratulations to Mayor Briana for allowing us to share her story. Her experience lives on within the Tasti D-Lite and Planet Smoothie social media training curriculum and now in this book. We can't put every customer on television to make up for our shortcomings, but it was fun in this case.

Going beyond will require an understanding that combining the competitive elements of these applications with fanatical customers can evoke some strong emotions—emotions that we need to understand and appreciate. So how do we move past the mechanics of these apps and really meet the needs and capture the hearts of our customers?

Here are five ways to go beyond the check-in:

1. **Get passionate about listening**. With the wealth of information now available online, getting visibility with the conversations happening around a business is critical. Five minutes a day can get you up to speed on what's happening, but the more time you can invest, the better your perspective will be. Use the tools that are available to set up alerts and notifications when certain activities occur.

2. **Play the game**. You need to download, sign up, claim your business, and get involved. How do you understand the dynamics of a community if you are not engaging within it yourself? Don't delegate that to someone else.

3. **Make it part of the DNA of your brand**. Impart this within your organization by pushing those insights and engaging with associates, suppliers, and customers online. You'll come up with some original and creative ideas for new campaigns, and everyone will be behind them. For example, the foursquare integration with our TastiRewards loyalty program was partly inspired by our active business and personal use of the foursquare application. At the end

of the day, the corporate culture needs to be able to support the online efforts. Push it from the inside out instead of needing to have customers educate you.

4. **Bridge the gap.** Why not bring the information into the physical location with a digital display? Many solutions exist that can display this interactive content, including mobile offers, check-ins, and mayorships. More on this later in the chapter.

5. **Don't make customer engagement a checklist.** Be prepared for spontaneous and human interaction around these technologies.

With Location Comes Humanization

We asked Asif Khan how he felt these location technologies are allowing us to become more human. He responded:

> Business has always been about the ability to listen and serve the customer. In a digital context, you're using these tools to listen and if done in the right way you are learning a lot about those individual consumers and respond to them and better meet their needs and interact with them. We look at location as a blending of all forms of media that could influence people. That includes digital signage, billboards and of course mobile devices. Now as a business owner, you have a digital archive of these conversations many of which are unsolicited. The reality is that they are doing it anyway. I think that the biggest investment a business has to make is to have someone who is socially listening, measuring and analyzing the data. That is the hire that has to happen in every business.

QR Codes

Among the more popular two-dimensional bar codes are quick response (QR) codes, which are an early step toward connecting mobile users to links, videos, and other interactive content by using the camera on users' smartphones. In addition, mobile payment applications are now using QR and other bar codes during transactions.

Imagine a teenager at a mall who can access a free song or ringtone by scanning a QR code on a billboard. Perhaps scanning a QR code at a museum would enhance your experience by directing you to a video tour or simply providing more information about a painting or an artist. QR codes can quickly and effectively transfer information and bridge the gap from what may be public to the very private and personal mobile device. Users can now take that information with them so they can access it in the future or share it with others.

You'll find a QR code for example on the back cover of this book. Powered by mobile marketing firm 44Doors (http://44doors.com), scanning this code with a QR code reader will direct your mobile browser to some interactive content.

In one study done by the CMB Consumer Pulse published in December 2011, 50 percent of smartphone users reported scanning a QR code. Magazines and newspapers were among the top sources of QR code scans. For nearly a fifth of those who scan, QR codes were part of the purchase process.[1]

One of our applications of this came in the form of QR codes on our tablet-based customer kiosks (aka TastiPads) where customers can use there smartphone to scan a QR code which directs their browser to a URL to receive more information. Some of the codes serve as a customer support function, and they can take with them the link to a flavor calendar or map of locations. From the social touch-point aspect, QR codes connect users to Facebook and Twitter thus allowing customers to connect.

Many people think this use of machine language will likely be replaced with the simple image capture of a product, location, or other data. Again, it's getting harder to know how much to invest in a given technology at any given time. It seems that what may be on the leading edge today could be in the technology recycling bin tomorrow. With adoption the key, keeping a close eye on customer behavior with these mobile technologies is critical. But how do you know what the customer behavior is if you don't implement the technology? Couldn't the adoption of a technology by businesses influence the adoption by consumers? Piloting the use of something new can be somewhat like the chicken and the egg game. Fortunately, many of these emerging technologies like QR codes can be tested on a low budget.

Augmented reality technologies already in use allow users to see social data or information left by others at a location or around a product. If the formula for adoption is convenience plus utility, it's just a matter of time until these mobile applications get greater traction in the marketplace.

Point of Sale: A Key Player

The great exchange in retail has always taken place at the cash register. What opportunities exist around providing more value and customer experience at this point? Exceeding expectations and removing any barriers like people and sales counters at this juncture are within reach, and it seems that new alternatives for point of sale (POS) are emerging daily.

Merchants are starting to bring the checkout to the sales floor with mobile POS solutions and tablets. With these devices, product and inventory information is close at hand, and so is the cash register with technologies like Square ready to handle credit card processing. Removing the journey to the counter means that customers are potentially that much closer to the sale. This should remind us of our discussion on getting in between the customer and the product in Chapter 5, "Don't Be Boring (and Other Thoughts on Relevance)."

We touch on socially enabled loyalty transactions and SNAP in Chapter 7, "Rolling with the Big Boys." As more functions of POS are extended beyond the simple sale, we'll start seeing more activity online related to what is actually happening inside the store.

The prospects for bringing virtual activity and conversation to the physical realm are just as great if not more mature.

Digital out of Home

Customer kiosks, interactive displays, and the like are starting to bring the virtual conversation into the real world. The emerging DOOH or digital-out-of-home industry offers many different solutions to bridge the gap between the virtual and the physical.

In our case, what is being said online about Tasti D-Lite can be valuable when it comes to educating customers in new markets. For example, comments from Twitter or reviews from Yelp can be shown on a live digital display for others to see. Beyond video and image slideshows, services like ScreenScape allow restaurants, retailers, hotels, gyms, and more to engage, inform, and entertain audiences with dynamic content. A web-based tool is used to manage what is pushed to the display.

New York City Times Square Tasti D-Lite franchise owner Bill Warshaw shares his experience. "The digital signage we use is a great presence and fits in well in the Times Square area with all the lights and buzz that is here. What it offers me is instantaneous access to the social activity and customers like the presence of the display. Seeing the Twitter feed encourages me to get more tweets and I want to do more with the concept."

Another example of tying these elements together with the brand is our Flavor Leaderboard application on Facebook that allows customers to "like" their favorite flavor and watch it move up the leaderboard. Customers can then optionally share their vote with others to perhaps encourage Facebook friends to help move that flavor up in the rankings. Designed to also be displayed within a location, customers can vote using the mobile browser on their smartphone. Here, their personal mobile device can drive what is seen on a public display. The current number one on the U.S. Tasti D-Lite Flavor Leaderboard? Cake batter.

Last, customer pole displays at the cash register can also be used to communicate social activity. Here again, the POS is being used as a social touch point. In this case, just about any kind of message and imagery can be displayed in a slideshow format right at the place customers typically look: at the pole display that shows how much they owe.

POS pole display: "Tasti Tweets" and other content are featured for customers to see.

The Heart of the Matter

When we start adding a very powerful ingredient like location to the online conversation, there is going to be an impact on the face-to-face conversation. Accountability at the line level starts with coming to the realization that the information is out there and what we do with it will speak volumes to associates and customers.

Accountability aside, the opportunity to recognize and celebrate with our customers is huge. Engaging emotionally is what most people are not ready for. This may not fit nicely into your policies and procedures but it seems that consumers are crossing the value threshold in new ways every day. We need to be prepared to boldly meet them there. If your customers are not engaging, perhaps the value exchange equation has not been satisfied.

These mobile and social technologies are feeding the desire that we have to connect—enabling us. It's no wonder that we get the shakes when we are separated from our technology. Our dependence on it has reached a level beyond anything we've experienced in the past.

Even with social champions in leadership, the last mile to the consumer needs to be shorter and we need to get there faster. The faster we connect and communicate, the greater the speed at which we can innovate together and progress as a species.

CHAPTER 10

Meet Your Cocreators

The secret is to gang up on the
problem, rather than each other.

*—Thomas Stallkamp, former Vice Chairman
and President, DaimlerChrysler*

One of the many ways that technology has impacted the brand-to-customer relationship is our ability to collaborate, cocreate, and support. The opportunities for getting customers actively involved in brand building and product development exercises are greater than ever, and, as you might have guessed, there are software solutions to help.

For most people, trusting customers as well as associates with the brand becomes the issue. For some people, ceding ownership is not even open for discussion. While the responsibility to protect and steward a brand certainly has not changed, embracing other people in the process of building that brand is a new reality for which few are prepared.

One of the popular misconceptions executives have is the belief that associates or customers would not actually participate in a positive manner and collaborate around brand initiatives. Assuming that they haven't had a prior bad experience, people employed by the company should certainly have a vested interest in the success of that which is contributing to their livelihood. Also if a business's services or products are of value to those using them, there should be little reason why they would not want to constructively engage with the brand to make the services or products better.

Democratization of the web has customers choosing how they interact, shape, and validate a product's image, and many times they can help drive where a company is going. By now we've all seen examples of this played out on the Internet. How does a business respond? Give the brand away and hope there is something left after the dust settles? What about the shareholders? If all we have left is the opportunity to influence the discussion, then how do we do that?

To be fair, we are coming at this from an uncommon perspective. As we allude to earlier, there is no doubt in our minds that Tasti D-Lite customers over the years have been strong advocates who, as a community, have in a significant way helped to define and carry the brand. In this case, the question might not be whether we trust them but whether they trust us with the brand.

In this chapter we start with some baby steps and then move toward some enterprise level solutions that can be used to support and empower those who are ready to embrace this mindset.

Embracing Field Agents

Customers aren't afraid to help merchants when it comes to the social and mobile tools they love to use. They want to see companies that they like embracing and taking part in the social space. Josh below brought to our attention a mapping issue with a foursquare venue which prevented users from checking in.

 Josh

@tastidlite Your map marker on foursquare for foursquare.com/v/tasti-dlite-... is placed in wrong state, ppl can't checkin to the official 4square spot

Field agent Josh: Customers who care enough will let you know when something is wrong.

This kind of feedback (via Twitter in this case) is valuable information. Josh effectively acted as a field agent, and thanks to his effort, he and others will be able to enjoy interacting with our Morganville, New Jersey, Tasti D-Lite location in the future.

As we see it, dismissing this kind of information would not only be silly, but it would be irresponsible. Why not simply listen, fix the problem, and thank the customer for the assistance? Once customers see that problems are resolved with their help, wouldn't that result in a deeper connection? We're obviously not going to intentionally create problems just so we can bond with customers. The point is that being willing to listen and accept their help is where we begin to lose control—in a good way.

The Power of a Question

Consider the restaurant chain P.F. Chang's. It poses creative questions on its Facebook page along with pictures to generate interaction but also to gain important insights. For example, a photo of a table setting will accompany the question, "What's wrong with this table setup?" Customers are challenged to engage by leaving a public comment, and P.F. Chang's gets the insights—perhaps information that it did not expect to receive. Having customers help create the content not only increases the interaction but as we discuss in Chapter 5, "Don't Be Boring (and Other Thoughts on Relevance)," it can have a positive effect on the search engine results as well.

Customers can detect an agenda. These simple straightforward questions bring down the walls, and the customers' defensive posture is relaxed. It is here that greater levels of intimacy can be enjoyed because of the absence of the hard sell or marketing jargon. Setting this tone allows customers to inject part of themselves into the product and brand. How the question is asked can say a great deal about the openness of a business and will also have a great deal to do with how the customer responds.

While it is not an issue in this case, for some people to even consider that customers might actually have something valuable to offer is a big step in the right direction.

Customers as Trainers

Our "Discovery Day" meetings with people interested in taking Tasti D-Lite and Planet Smoothie to different parts of the country and the world include a demonstration of our use of social media. What happens when you solicit followers to help show some prospective master franchisees how Twitter works? It's a risky exercise perhaps, but only if you don't know how engaged the community is.

Tasti D-Lite
@tastidlite

Getting ready to show some friends from UAE Twitter.
Please say hello so they can see how this works!

Julia Roy
@juliaroy

@tastidlite Hello tasti friends. I'm going to eat you!

Tasti trainers: Julia responds to show how Twitter works.

The results? In less than nine minutes, a potential of 180,000 impressions were generated on Twitter through just eight responses as influential users like @juliaroy, @ginidietrich, and @anamitra joined the conversation. This large number represents the number of followers that could have potentially seen the comments. While Twitter has since changed the level of visibility these kinds of responses can have, it should be clear that the investment we had made in the Twitter community allowed us to draw from it when needed.

We're not saying that this sealed the deal for our new master franchisees in the UAE, but locations are now open in Dubai and Abu Dhabi. They can be found on Facebook at http://facebook.com/tastidliteUAE.

Customers as Informants

Empowering customers with access and information does a number of things. From a product and customer service perspective, a connected consumer can help keep us more accountable at the retail level. The following is a good example of such an opportunity.

Kenlie
@ALLTHEWEIGH

First time I've ever been disappointed with @tastidlite...

Tasti D-Lite
@tastidlite

@ALLTHEWEIGH Anything we can help with?

Kenlie
@ALLTHEWEIGH

@tastidlite Nah...the guy was just a big jerk so I left. I've had over 100 pleasant experiences there so this being the first isn't too bad...

Kenlie reaches out: Insights of all kinds come from online discussions.

More detail came as a result of our follow-up tweets. In this case, our disappointed friend reached out on her channel of choice and included the @tastidlite mention, which (we think she knew) would certainly catch our attention. From there, we could pass along the information about a problem to the appropriate party.

Defending the Brand

Customers want to help because they care. If they did not care, they would simply go elsewhere and not worry about solving a problem related to a product or service they love.

If an online reviewer is creating content that is unfair or unconstructive, customers have been known to come to the defense of the brand. If they see a business trying to help solve a problem, unreasonable or undeserved complaints are swiftly called out by others in most of the popular communities.

As we mention in Chapter 1, "Introduction to a Tasti Story," this can and will happen regardless of a corporate presence. Building a community in the right way around these advocates can serve as a strong network of empowered brand owners.

This Is Going to Get Sticky

Removing layers and inviting customers into processes that will help find the next version of a product or service can provide an emotional buy-in that cannot be created otherwise. The level of engagement and resulting stickiness for that consumer going forward can be extraordinary.

Imagine, for example, a customer who took part in helping name or develop a new Tasti D-Lite flavor. The next time that customer walks past a store with a friend, you can bet there will be some excitement involved as they feel the pride of ownership in the brand.

Again, creating the sticky effect requires a loosening of control, but the net gain is worth the loss because it results in a level of commitment that is greater for that customer.

Taking It to the Crowd

As new tools for online collaboration continue to develop, customers are becoming more involved in potential decisions as companies are opening up and looking for not only feedback but design and marketing input. Crowdsourcing takes groupthink to another level with idea sharing, voting, and debating about the best ideas and concepts.

People want to help, even if they don't really care about a product or brand; their desire to help others or to make something right can be seen on a regular basis. This has been happening since the first electronic bulletin boards and online forums appeared.

Name That Mascot

After inheriting a wily mascot and costume from Planet Smoothie named Cup Man in late 2011, we thought it would be appropriate to create and name a mascot for Tasti D-Lite. Aside from the great potential for some creative interaction between the two characters, we figured this would be a good way to help develop the personalities of each brand. The challenge quickly became what to name the new Tasti D-Lite mascot.

Our Name that Mascot contest on Facebook would help us choose a name that would best represent the brand image. Customers submitting names would also have the opportunity to provide a rationale as to why the name fit. A panel of distinguished judges at the home office would choose the winner and award prizes.

Who am I?: Customers help name the new Tasti D-Lite mascot.

Our vice president of marketing, Donna Smith, shared her thoughts on why we should allow customers to participate this way. "By encouraging customers to submit names for the mascot, we are able to gain important insight into how they are perceiving the brand. The other benefit I see is that this enables the customer to take ownership of the brand in a way that is very low risk for the company."

The winner? Fillmore Cups. The customer's rationale? "This name would be perfect for the Tasti D-Lite mascot because it represents the growing demand for Tasti D-Lite and wild popularity of this wonderful healthy dessert chain. I want to go fill my cup right now!!"

On the final name selection, Donna offers, "It's perfect. Fillmore will be touring Tasti stores across the country, generating excitement around the brand and helping franchisees to 'fill more cups' with delicious, healthier soft-serve."

It's interesting to see how customers can come up with concepts and ideas that someone sitting on the other side of the brand might not conceive of. Remove the marketing filter, and the gates are wide open. Some of the other creative submissions we received are shown in the table below.

NAME	CUSTOMER RATIONALE
D-Lish	Because Tasti D-Lite treats are DELICIOUS!!!!!
Stanley Swirl	Tasti D-Lite is a sweet swirl in a cup! And he looks like a Stanley :)
D Mixmaster	D for D-Lite and Mixmaster for all the different flavors Tasti D offers.
Vinny Vanilla	He's vanilla! Plus this way you can have other characters like Charles Chocolate.
Sprinkles	Sprinkles is not only a cute name, but it will also increase sales. People will want to buy more toppings when they think of the name.
Litening	"Litening" would be pronounced the same as "Lightning." The name fits with the mission and name of the store. Plus, lightning has a neat effect, just like Tasti D-Lite.
Yummi-D	I think it's important to you to use attributes of the company's name, Tasti D-Lite, in the mascot's name so people know who he represents.

Other Sources of Innovation

New customer-centric solutions and applications are being used to collaborate directly with customers on a greater scale than existed before. Whether that's garnering feedback, harvesting new ideas, or helping to drive innovations, platforms now exist for those brave enough to use them.

Our friend Boris Pluskowski offers this; "Innovation is all about problem solving. It's about identifying the key problems that are stopping the company from achieving its strategic aims, strategic goals, and finding better and new ways in which to solve those problems. Modern day companies are realizing that the next big innovation in their company can come from anywhere. Additionally, the process and discipline around creating new things has value, it is repeatable, it can be sustainable, and it can be driven."

For many, the suggestion box in the break room or at the retail counter has been the extent of that process and discipline. The ability to reach out and engage hundreds of thousands of people inside and outside a company is now within reach. Customers, associates, suppliers, and anyone with an interest can learn about challenges within an organization and then use the tools to help solve those problems. While daunting perhaps, tapping into that intellectual capital on a large scale should appear to have value for most businesses.

Are All Customers Created Equal?

Understanding that different kinds of customers can provide different kinds of insights and benefits is critical. Again, Boris offers his expertise in this area:

> One of the things I tell my clients is that you want to look beyond your current customers. Current customers are only going to give you one thing: iterations of your existing products. The reason why is because they're

not dissatisfied with the product. They love the product, so they don't really want to change it. They may want to add bits and pieces to it, but that's all. If you want to find the next big thing, you have to move up the dissatisfaction scale.

Next up on the dissatisfaction scale is the so-called lead user or lead adopter. These are the people who are only buying your product because it's the closest thing to what they really want to buy, it just doesn't exist yet. They use it, they buy it, and they adapt and they change it. If you ask the lead user, they'll probably give you the next generation of your product.

If you really want to go far out, the people you need to ask are people who aren't your customers at all. These are the people who are so unsatisfied, you have absolutely nothing to offer them and they don't even want to touch you. They're the ones that can give you the real future of your company. So, my mantra is always, current customers are going to give you iterations, lead users are going to give you generations, and non-customers are going to give you the future.

Follow-Through

Once all the feedback and collaboration is in, it's time to act. Perhaps some people are afraid to ask for feedback and collaboration because they know that they will have to implement as a result. In our mascot example above, what's the worst that could happen? Our mascot ends up with a crazy name?

Boris offers, "One client we had did an employee challenge to come up with new names for the conference rooms at the corporate office. Employees engaged and came up with really good names, but the company felt the result was trivial and didn't take the exercise further."

Asking for ideas without any kind of focus can bring frustration for all parties involved. Using best practices around a little targeted collaboration will help establish some boundaries and expectations. Capturing ideas that are both relevant and implementable should be the objective. In this case, you come away with something creative that has a purpose and is valued by the audience.

Members of the audience will not expect all their ideas to be implemented, but when associates and customers can actually see a result from the process, they are more likely to stay engaged and contribute in the future. When nothing happens, the crowd will stop participating.

The Heart of the Matter

Giving control to those people using and consuming a product or service is never easy. Just about every discipline within an organization is going to have issues with making customers part of the brand-building process. Here is where the champion in the C-suite needs to effectively communicate and drive the cultural changes necessary to stay relevant in the marketplace.

If people really care about a product and wish the best for it, embracing their input would seem reasonable. Balancing that with where the brand needs to be in the future is just one of the challenges we face on this side of the business.

CHAPTER 11

The Social Future

> It is a paradox that in our time of drastic rapid change, when the future is in our midst devouring the present before our eyes, we have never been less certain about what is ahead of us.
> —*Eric Hoffer, author (1902–1983)*

W hat is the future of consumer behavior and how will it drive the adoption of new technologies? We won't be in a position to take that journey unless we know our customers. We'll need to know a bit about the shiny new toys they play with as well. In this last chapter we talk with some industry friends and partners who have been around the block a few times when it comes to new technologies, loyalty, and transparency. There are some fundamentals that haven't changed (and hopefully won't), but everything else is up for debate. We start with privacy.

Privacy and the Value Exchange

In Chapter 9, "The Location Business," we talk about the privacy thresholds that consumers are willing to cross when there is something of value to be had. As it relates to the sharing of personal information, what does the future hold as the next generation of digital natives enters the marketplace and workforce?

As more social and location-based applications and services offer greater value for consumers, views on privacy will continue to shift. Founder and president of computer services franchise Data Doctors Ken Colburn has been observing the behavior and trends around consumer electronics for many years. We asked him about changes in privacy, and he responded: "When you grow up sharing everything about your life, your psychological need to keep things from others diminishes because you live transparently. This shift will continue to have its negative implications, but more so for those that didn't grow up with it. Eventually, this transparent way of engaging will drift up to the C-suites of corporate America, which is where the real changes will occur."

One example of a service currently providing this value exchange is HopStop. If you need point-to-point walking, biking, or mass-transit directions in New York City or in over 100 other cities, this free location-based service can help. HopStop relies on location information voluntarily shared by users to provide targeted offers from advertisers who are nearby or perhaps even in the path of your travels. This HopStop feature is similar to the foursquare specials that we cover earlier, but HopStop differs in that it has more information about your trip, for example, where you are heading and what time you are expected to pass a business advertising on the service. We asked HopStop CEO Joe Meyer about this value exchange. He says, "We believe this is a fair exchange of information, and one the end user is comfortable with as there's a value proposition for both the user and the provider of the service. The serving of ads within popular location-based services such as HopStop is a far more natural experience, and users are more comfortable receiving geotargeted messaging."

Where the core service is dependent upon the location information, it makes sense to use those data to make more relevant offers available to users. Consumers get a valuable (and free) service, advertisers are reaching those nearby, and neither party is unfairly taking advantage of the other.

Let's take this a step further. If we can make our location known through our mobile devices and objects like billboards or even moving objects can be geotagged (implanted with a location identifier), then relationships can be established between them. In other words, when location data are available for all these people, places, and things, there is great opportunity to engage or influence users.

We met Asif Khan, founder and president of the Location Based Marketing Association, in an earlier chapter. His perspective? "We're already putting devices on our children in the event we need to find them. We are at the point of choosing to share this information to receive something in return like a connection to others and to find something of value possibly through an opt-in to certain subject matter."

Asif continues, "Picture a moving object like a bus with digital signage on it that is geotagged. Now add individuals who have made their whereabouts known and their demographic information is stored. We're in a situation where the content on that moving display can be rendered based on the context of other objects nearby. In other words, a personalized ad, offer, or some social messaging can be displayed to potentially influence the individual. You understand me, and therefore what I am seeing is potentially valuable or relevant to me."

Another example relates to the future of personal and business networking. Connecting with just the right person or resource at the right time can be invaluable. Let's say we check in or otherwise disclose our whereabouts at an event. LinkedIn is already in a position to connect us with the most relevant attendees based on our professional profile information. Recommendations provided by LinkedIn based on our business interests would potentially link us in a very human way and make for some powerful and efficient networking. The technology components already exist, but we're not quite there yet.

As our behavioral intelligence profile grows, marketers will have more information with which to interact. Mobilize that data, and powerful things can happen. Joe Meyer says, "I envision the lines between behavioral and location-based targeting blurring over the next few years to become one and the same."

Dynamic examples like this are already starting to appear. How we design positive experiences around these technologies will determine the level of success we will have as marketers. Here Asif says, "Content is king, but how we are going to experience and engage with that content? It's only activation that is going to make it awesome."

Great experiences will come only when security and privacy expectations have been properly managed and relationships have been well defined. Step outside the parameters that consumers have established, and trust will be lost.

Dave Matthews is senior vice president and chief information officer for the National Restaurant Association. We asked him what the future holds as it relates to privacy. Dave offers, "Digital natives so far have expressed far less concern over privacy issues than they have over 'look and feel' and usability changes to mobile applications and websites. This is bound to change as more digital natives enter the workforce and become more aware of these issues. Digital privacy is far more complex than simply identity and content. The legislative and judicial branches of our government are only now addressing these issues at the fringe. Digital natives and digital aliens will need to educate themselves quickly before they abrogate rights through inaction and inattentiveness."

The Personalized Experience

Businesses taking advantage of more targeted and valuable exchanges will not only be seen as more relevant, but they will do it more cost effectively than ever. Simultaneously, however, channel management will become a greater challenge. Bill Hanifin is managing director of Hanifin Loyalty, a U.S.-based marketing agency focused on delivering customer strategy and business intelligence solutions to its clients. He says, "Most brand conversations take place today outside of traditional channels, and brands need to connect the dots between nontransactional points of interaction between consumers and their brand in order to influence future purchase behavior." Already we are managing social network pages and profiles simply to post content, have conversations, and build and support relationships. Future transactions will come at other points and through other channels only as trust and affinity are established.

The prospects for businesses to be proactive are growing daily. Bill continues, "Loyalty marketing has traditionally worked 'behind the transaction'; that is, marketers were analyzing the results of historical transaction records and then offering up a value proposition based on that behavior to influence future purchases. The new opportunity that exists is for brands to 'get ahead of the transaction,' insert themselves into the conversations taking place across many social channels, and, in a sincere and transparent manner, demonstrate to consumers their value."

A simple example of a personalized experience is our Tasti Flavor Alerts. This service was the brainchild of Planet Tasti vice president of global development, Kurt Ullman, who recognized the passion that customers had around their favorite Tasti D-Lite flavors. Launched in 2009, Flavor Alerts are an e-mail and SMS (Short Message Service) text service designed to notify (and entice) fans when their favorite flavor is "on tap." Customers can sign up by location to receive alerts for a specific flavor or for a list of all the featured flavors. They can opt in to receive other offers if they'd like. Otherwise customer information will be used only to let customers know when their favorite awaits.

One blogger wrote about these Flavor Alerts as follows: "Just when you thought frozen dessert couldn't get any easier, Tasti has announced Flavor Alerts. Got a favorite flave—no problem—let them know and you'll be notified via text when it's featured. Want to know what's on tap at your local frozen paradise? Just check your email. Forget that these alerts are like the crack dealer who knows where you live and buzzes you to see if you need more rock, I love it. Tasti is my rock, and I look forward to the text that reads: CHOCOLATE NY CHEESECAKE & PEANUT BUTTER FUDGE. XO TDL."[1]

Flavor Alerts allow us to offer a fun and interactive element around the flavor offerings to our most regular and loyal customers. It also provides us with some valuable flavor and delivery preference information so we can make better and more relevant marketing decisions down to the store level.

Susanne Goldstone
@susqhb

@tastidlite Your flavor alerts just might change my life.

Flavor Alerts: Life changers?

Periodically, customers will reply to these automated messages. Two of the standout e-mail responses we received are, "I am sitting outside hoping you open soon :-)" and "Toasted Coconut Cookie HERE I COME!"

Social Loyalty

As we say in the beginning of this book, there is no final destination when it comes to customer loyalty. The dynamic customer journey coupled with changes in technology have businesses trying to hit a moving target and the desire of consumers to receive tangible rewards and personal recognition for their loyalty has not changed. Smart marketers are taking these elements online and leveraging the viral nature of social networking. New elements like gaming also come into play. So just what does a social-friendly loyalty program of the future look like?

Concerning this, Bill Hanifin says,

> My early definition of social loyalty is a data driven incentive structure that provides an environment through which shoppers share information, opinions and recommendations, impacting future purchase decisions. Through this model, brands will continue to evolve in the ways they can engage with their existing and potential customers "ahead of the transaction."
>
> I also see that a social-friendly program will have customer engagement as the "tip of the spear" and will seek to drive purchase behavior across a life cycle value chain, rather than focusing on singular objectives (e.g., acquisition or retention). Social loyalty will communicate its value in context of the customer experience and will allow individual merchants to engage customers via mobile devices and in proximity to merchant location.
>
> The mix of rewards we are used to seeing in loyalty programs will shift as well, with an accelerating shift away from deferred savings towards large rewards and with more emphasis on rewards that speak immediacy, spontaneity, and excitement. The opportunity for brands taking smart steps to develop what we term as social loyalty programs has tremendous and obvious potential.

When users interact online, games are not far behind. Add mobility to the mix, and the sky is the limit when it comes to the "gamification" of social and location-based applications. Customer behavior is being rewarded for all kinds of online, mobile, and location-based activity around brands and products. Throw in a little competition with badges and a leaderboard, and you've got a recipe for some great individual as well as shared experiences. These game-based mechanisms for influencing behavior are already starting to make an impact within loyalty programs. As we discuss in Chapter 7, "Rolling with the Big Boys," adding these kinds of features and benefits within traditional programs can help drive adoption of those programs among consumers.

Fundamentals

So what has all this really done for us and other businesses? What new principles have we learned and need to put into practice going forward? If the playing field has been leveled and we've removed a layer of corporate speak, influence, and control, then what is left is what we have always had—the fundamentals. Stripping away these things has amplified and exposed the fundamental business components and processes that we're in business for to begin with. The sooner we can go through and embrace the process and journey of transparency, the sooner we can meet the needs of our customers through a greater focus on the core elements of our business.

What hasn't changed? We asked Ken Colburn this question, and he responded with, "At its core, the social and mobile revolutions are simply a shift in communication protocols that actually get us back to our small-town roots. In small towns, we all know each other and what's happening to whom. Social media is simply expanding the size of our individual 'small towns.' Engaging with your customers as you would if you were in a small town is the opportunity and *the key* to transitioning your business from a cold, faceless facade to a warm, human connection."

David Matthews offers his perspective: "The fundamentals of the restaurant industry will not change; delivery of quality product by caring and dedicated staff to create a dining experience that makes the customer feel like a guest. The manner in which this experience is created and delivered may change but not the fundamental reason consumers like to dine in restaurants and restaurateurs enjoy their industry."

The Social-Friendly Enterprise

Social media is rapidly moving from adoption to full integration for both consumers and businesses. While some businesses are still sitting on the sidelines, many are beyond testing the waters and are now refining their processes and voice. Five fundamentals or attributes of the social-friendly enterprise of the future are:

1. **The ability to *listen effectively.*** We cover this in Chapter 2, "The Race for Transparency," and elsewhere. Understanding the opportunities online begins with education, and you can't learn anything with your mouth open. Sharp ears and a desire to impart the virtual perspective of the customer within an organization is just the beginning.
2. **The ability to *engage creatively.*** Capturing the heart of consumers means meeting them where they are. Sometimes you can't wait for them to come to you, so get creative. We hope we have demonstrated to you that there is no box to think outside of.
3. **The ability to *execute locally.*** Accountability at the local level will continue to be something that businesses deal with on multiple fronts. Be prepared to offer a consistent experience between your online presence and offline activities. In the future, all customer-facing systems and applications will have social elements. Use the technology to bridge the virtual-physical or personal-to-public gap. We touch on this in Chapter 9, "The Location Business."

4. **The ability to *embrace transparency*.** Social media gives consumers a glimpse into the culture and people behind the products and services they love. What does that picture look like for your organization? As we cover in Chapter 3, "Going Behind the Brand," this starts with the individuals behind the brand.

5. **The ability to *curate and tell your stories*.** Capturing and sharing the moments and experiences you are having with customers will touch others inside and outside your organization. Data and numbers will provide the rational justification; stories will provide the emotional connection. Don't underestimate the power of either when it comes to influencing the various personalities occupying the C-suite.

A Silver Bullet?

Is social media a silver bullet? Short answer: no. Social media is simply a channel. Perhaps more accurately it is many dynamic and powerful channels through which consumers are communicating.

On this subject, we liked what John Havens, executive vice president of strategy and engagement for Yoxi, had to say; "There is no silver bullet with social media. When clients have said to me in the past, 'I want a Facebook page,' my response has always been the same, 'Tell me about your business objectives.' Only then can we talk about the channels that are going to support those objectives and what the calls to action should be for your customers. We can layer in these great new tools, but the focus always needs to go back to the product or service we provide."

A Social Media Bubble?

Will the social media bubble pop? Short answer: no. A "bubble" suggests that there has been an expansion of the use of

social technologies. While this is certainly the case, the level of integration within traditional business systems and processes is significant. Also, consumer behavior and adoption of these networks and technologies show no sign of slowing down.

We asked Ken Colburn this question, and he answered, "As with most new sectors of our economy, the 'bubble of irrational exuberance' will always exist, but the lessons of the dot-com era are helping to keep the social media bubble from getting too big. The inability to predict the true impact of any new technology has always made it more speculative, which helps to create bubbles of various sizes. Social funding sites like Kickstarter are changing how things get funded for start-ups, so demonstrating the fundamentals before institutional investors step in is getting easier."

And David Matthews offers: "There is a bubble to the extent that there will be vendor/company consolidation as business models fail to gain traction or differentiate themselves from their competition. However, social media has taken root across multiple generations and will continue to grow and develop over time. There will certainly be changes as businesses consolidate, merge, and morph, but we will always be able to trace back to the founding innovators."

The Legal Department of the Future

One of the great mysteries we've always struggled with is what to do with the legal department. Kidding aside, our attorney friends are faced with the same forces of change that are impacting the rest of the organization. Working together to solve new challenges in an increasingly open and social workplace and marketplace will require conscious effort from both sides. The opportunity for the executive team is to invite the legal department to the discussion early. Reaching out during the concept phase of a project will not only save valuable time later, but it can help impart the vision across disciplines.

It goes both ways, however. Our own general counsel Grayson Brown offers:

> The general counsel needs to earn the right to be invited into that dialogue. He's going to do that by being proactive and being someone who is adding value by bringing solutions to the conversation and someone who is not going to just throw up obstacles. Understand the opportunity, allow it to drive the business, and be diligent to review the areas of risk. In order to do that, you have to be involved to the point that you know what is going on. You are going to have to be more diligent about developing those relationships with the marketing department and others who are engaging customers. Our involvement in the business has to be magnified to the point where the relationship between the business folks and the lawyers is unrecognizable. You are going to need to be able to take your legal training and leverage it for business results. Attorneys need to be willing to put themselves into the stream of the business, which may not feel natural to them.

We're pretty sure this is not what our attorney friends were programmed to do in law school, but things are changing. In fact, some companies are deploying "mini-GCs" in different business units to both accelerate learning for the attorneys and deliver better service to clients.[2]

When we asked about the legal developments we are going to see between employers and employees, Grayson said, "We are going to continue to see consternation as it relates to use of social media in the workplace and in the hiring process but we will also see new privacy laws that bring clarity to the process and will enable businesses to be more nimble in both hiring and firing."

As a whole, legal services are becoming commoditized as resources like LegalZoom gain popularity on the Internet and more information is available to consumers and businesses.

Grayson continues, "We're going to see a huge shift in the legal profession. The attorney of the future is going to have to become more human driven through relationships and more niche driven and be able to bring those together to advance his craft and discipline and ultimately his career. But the only thing that will keep it alive is the human element."

Incidentally, Grayson has been the mayor of our home office venue on foursquare for many months. Attorneys can be very competitive.

Tasti D-lite HQ
341 Cool Springs Blvd Suite 100, Franklin, Tennessee 37067
Office (Edit)

Mayor: Grayson B.
32 check-ins in last 60 days

General counsel as mayor: Even attorneys can play the game.

Being able to respond to the needs of the market is all about being integrated within the organization. At the macro level, this applies to the various types of business models and formats.

The Future of Franchising

In Chapter 2, "The Race for Transparency," we touch on the advantage and the changing face of franchising. Along with other business models, the franchise industry as a whole will continue to be challenged in new ways. How we structure relationships will determine how well we face new opportunities together in the future.

About the conflicting needs for brand control and localized content, International Franchise Association president and CEO Steve Caldeira says:

It's certainly going to continue to evolve. Each franchise system is different, but those that listen, act swiftly, and stay on their toes about changes in technology and changes in customers' perceptions of the brand, those will be the companies that rise to the top in the future. The main thing is that the roles need to be clearly defined, albeit with room for adjustments as they warrant as new social networks or technologies burst onto the scene. Social media policies should be part of the conversation with franchisees as soon as they are brought into a new system (and oftentimes should be part of the discussions franchise development professionals are having with prospects before they are brought into a system). The policies should have input from the legal department, marketing and communications departments, advertising, and others, because social media ultimately touches every facet of a franchise business.

What Does the Future Hold?

So what can we expect in the future? We close with these eight thoughts:

1. **Privacy as we know it will continue to diminish.** Personal data will be more readily shared and made available, especially as advertisers provide greater value in exchange.
2. **User-generated content will continue to get more granular.** We've already moved beyond people, places, and things to sharing images, experiences, and more. The level of detail and activity around the products that we buy and services we use will get more dynamic.
3. **Understanding the context of the social conversation will grow in importance** (related to item 2). The details will be the downfall of those not listening effectively.
4. **Integration of social and traditional systems and processes will continue.** Loyalty programs, point of sale,

digital displays, CRM, and navigation systems, among many others have already embraced social elements.

5. **Consolidation of social networks, applications, and services will continue.**

6. **Location will become part of every social interaction.** Content is king, but content with location is even more powerful.

7. **Curation and brand journalism will grow in popularity as more brands include reporting and storytelling in their content strategies.**

8. **Mobile devices will continue to reshape every level of commerce ranging from location-based service to mobile payments to augmented reality.** Mobile devices will receive greater focus from brick-and-mortar organizations where they will have the biggest impact.

The Heart of the Matter

What does the future hold? We believe that the future is human. To be more specific, the future is more human. All the ingredients are in place, and as much as we allow it, we'll be able to connect with others in real and meaningful ways as we seek mutually beneficial exchanges.

In life and in technology, ill-defined relationships breed problems and confusion. This will become a greater issue as more information is offered by consumers and is put to use by marketers. In addition, expectations around privacy need to be managed very carefully.

Social media is setting apart great companies. Through this, we'll see more clearly, listen better, and hopefully change faster. What impact will we have as we pursue these opportunities with the right motives? Beyond enriching the lives of others by providing great products and services, lasting experiences will follow if we are able to break through to new levels.

We hope this section of each chapter has been helpful if not challenging to you both personally and professionally. Moving the needle within our minds, hearts, and organizations can be difficult. As we write these final lines on Easter Sunday 2012, we have great hope for what is ahead in life and in business—hope for our economy, for our country, and for our world.

The future is human, so bring your heart with you.

NOTES

Prologue

1. Kara Ohngren, "How Tasti D-Lite Finds Success with Social Media," *Entrepreneur Magazine*, December 19, 2011, http://www .entrepreneur.com/article/222444.

Chapter 1

1. Ellen Byron, "Tasti D-Lite Banks on Its Fanatical Fans for Growth," *Wall Street Journal*, July 29, 2008, http://online.wsj .com/article/SB121729652087692073.html.
2. Marian Burros, "Fewer Calories Than Ice Cream, but More Than You Think," *New York Times*, October 2, 2002, http://www .nytimes.com/2002/10/02/dining/fewer-calories-than-ice-cream -but-more-than-you-think.html.
3. Facebook, "Tasti-D Rules My Life" group, http://www.facebook .com/group.php?gid=2213369385, accessed December 12, 2011.
4. Marie Lyn Bernard, The Gospel of Tasti D-Lite, July 28, 2006, http://marielynbernard.blogspot.com/2006/07/i-dont-need -permission-i-make-my-own.html.
5. Sam D, Tasti D-Lited: Flavors, reviews, http://tastidlited .blogspot.com/.
6. Annette Simmons, *Whoever Tells the Best Story Wins* (New York: Amacom, May 9, 2007).

Chapter 2

1. Wikipedia, "User Generated Content," http://en.wikipedia.org/ wiki/User-generated_content, accessed February 3, 2012.
2. Mainstay Salire, "The Power of Going Local: Comparing the Impact of Corporate Versus Local Facebook Pages," white paper sponsored by Hearsay Social, San Mateo, CA, http://info .hearsaysocial.com/rs/hearsaysocial/images/Hearsay-Corporate -to-local.pdf, accessed April 1, 2012.

Chapter 3

1. Wikipedia, "Disparate Treatment," http://en.wikipedia.org/wiki/Disparate_treatment, accessed January 13, 2012.
2. Kate Trgovac, Fear and Loathing in Social Media, Slideshare presentation, November 23, 2009, http://www.slideshare.net/mynameiskate/fear-and-loathing-in-social-media-2561711.
3. C. V. Harquail, What's a Brandividual?, Authentic Organizations Blog, May 20, 2009, http://authenticorganizations.com/harquail/2009/05/20/whats-a-brandividual/.
4. David Armano, The Age of Brandividualism, Experience Matters Blog, January 23, 2009, http://experiencematters.criticalmass.com/2009/01/23/the-age-of-brandividualism/.
5. John Biggs, "A Dispute Over Who Owns a Twitter Account Goes to Court," *New York Times*, December 25, 2011, http://www.nytimes.com/2011/12/26/technology/lawsuit-may-determine-who-owns-a-twitter-account.html?_r=2.

Chapter 4

1. EMarketer, "When Consumers Tweet Complaints, Should Brands Respond?," Emarketer.com, October 26, 2011, http://www.emarketer.com/Article.aspx?R=1008659.
2. Catherine Ridings, David Gefen, and Bay Arinze, "Psychological Barriers: Lurker and Poster Motivation and Behavior in Online Communities," Communications of the Association for Information Systems, http://aisel.aisnet.org/cais/vol18/iss1/16/, accessed February 3, 2012.

Chapter 5

1. Wikipedia, "Social Media Optimization," http://en.wikipedia.org/wiki/Social_media_optimization, accessed February 5, 2012.
2. Twitter, "Promoted Trends," https://business.twitter.com/en/advertise/promoted-trends/, accessed March 15, 2012.
3. NBC, *30 Rock*, season 4, episode 1 (originally aired October 15, 2009).
4. Rick Liebling, "TastiDLite—Supporting Social Media with Human Interaction," *Eyecube*, January 21, 2009, http://eyecube.wordpress.com/2009/01/21/tastidlite-supporting-social-media-with-human-interaction/.
5. PRSA staff, #PRin2012: 12 Trends That Will Change Public Relations, PRSAY Newsletter, December 19, 2011, http://prsay.prsa.org/index.php/2011/12/19/12-trends-for-public-relations-in-2012/.

Chapter 7

1. Jennifer Van Grove, "40 of the Best Twitter Brands and the People Behind Them," Mashable, January, 21, 2009, http://mashable.com/2009/01/21/best-twitter-brands/.
2. Blumpo, "Frequently Asked Questions," http://blumpo.com/index.php/questions/, accessed March 1, 2012.
3. Ibid.

Chapter 8

1. Matthew S., Yelp, http://www.yelp.com/biz/tasti-dlite-new-york -2, accessed February 13, 2012.
2. Loren, "Tasti D-What?" She's Still Hungry: A Foodie Newsletter, August 7, 2011, http://shesstillhungry.blogspot.com/2011/08/tasti-d-what.html, accessed June 5, 2012.

Chapter 9

1. Chadwick Martin Bailey, Nine Things to Know About Consumer Behavior and QR Codes, cmbinfo.com, http://blog.cmbinfo.com/qr-codes/, accessed April 2, 2012.

Chapter 11

1. Elizabeth, Code Tasti, Please Judge Me, December 10, 2008, http://pleasejudgeme.blogspot.com/2008/12/code-tasti.html.
2. Shannon Green, "In-House Lawyers Increasingly in Dual Legal/Business Roles," Law.com, March 9, 2012, http://www.law.com/jsp/cc/PubArticleCC.jsp?id=1202544912017.

GLOSSARY

backchannel: In terms of social networking, the backchannel is the real-time online conversation and activity taking place in the virtual realm during a physical event.

badge: Within various social networks and applications, badges are virtual objects that users can earn for certain behavior or activity. These objects are collected and typically displayed within the user's profile.

Best Swirl Contest: During Tweetups or other Tasti D-Lite parties, contestants compete to create the most aesthetically pleasing Tasti D-Lite cup or cone. Judges vote to determine the winner.

brand journalism: Brand journalism is the art of using storytelling to make companies seem more human and accessible to their customers.

crowdsourcing: A method or process of distributed collaboration or outsourcing that allows shared thoughts or work to contribute to a cause or solution.

cultural autonomy: Within an organization, this term describes an environment in which the culture is allowed to develop and mature organically.

Day at Tasti: An internal home-office program designed to help associates learn more about the Tasti D-Lite customer experience, products, equipment, and technology.

digital natives: The generation of individuals that has grown up with social technologies, mobile devices, and the Internet.

digital out of home (DOOH): A term used to describe the industry that provides digital display solutions outside the home.

Discovery Day: During the franchise development process, candidates interested in franchise ownership attend a one-day Discovery Day meeting at the Tasti D-Lite home office in Franklin, Tennessee.

disparate treatment: A potential form of discrimination in the hiring process, disparate treatment could apply if online profiles are used as qualifiers, and less than favorable treatment is given to those without such profiles.

earned media: Favorable publicity or media coverage. Earned in the sense that it is not paid for, created, or owned by the individual or organization receiving the publicity or coverage.

EdgeRank: The method or algorithm that Facebook uses to display posts within a user's stream. EdgeRank is based on relevance and interaction with the content published by others.

Flavor Leaderboard: A Facebook application that allows users to vote for their favorite Tasti D-Lite flavor. The leaderboard displays the popularity ranking of each flavor.

flavors of the day: In Tasti D-Lite locations, the flavors of the day are those flavors "on-tap" and ready to be dispensed from soft-serve machines.

fro-yo: Frozen yogurt.

gamification: The use of gaming elements and design techniques within applications to encourage user behavior, interaction, and adoption.

geotagging: The practice or method of adding location information to virtual objects such as files or images. For example, a Facebook wall post could optionally contain a location identifier.

hashtag: A character (#) used on Twitter (or other social networks) that is followed by a keyword that ties posts together for search purposes.

IRL: Acronym for "in real life."

location-based service (LBS): A service that utilizes location-based technologies, such as geotagging, to include location data within applications or programs.

mashing up: The linking or promoting of online content in order to increase the visibility of such content.

mayorship: A designation held by the "mayor" of a foursquare venue. The mayor is the user who has the greatest number of current check-ins at a particular location.

mayor special: A foursquare special that is configured to reward the mayor of a particular venue.

owned media: Published media such as a blog, website, or social feed that are created and controlled by a user or organization.

promoted tweet: One of Twitter's forms of business advertising, promoted tweets can appear at the top of relevant search results pages on twitter.com.

quick response (QR) code: One of the most popular two-dimensional bar codes, QR codes contain information that can be scanned by a bar code reader application on mobile devices.

RickRolling: A practical joke that involves tricking an unsuspecting person into watching the Rick Astley video *Never Gonna Give You Up*.

search engine optimization (SEO): The method or process used to improve the organic visibility of web content within search engines.

social CRM: An extension of typical customer relationship management functions that are designed to include monitoring, engagement, and online community management.

swarm special: An offer within foursquare that becomes available only or is unlocked when a certain number of users check-in at a particular venue within a specified period of time.

Tasti Flavor Alert: SMS (short message service) text or e-mail message that alerts subscribers when their favorite Tasti D-Lite flavor is "on tap."

Tasti Healthy Habit Search: A campaign launched in 2011 designed to identify, connect with, and potentially reward customers who have benefited from adding Tasti D-Lite to their healthy lifestyles.

Tasti TreatCard: A two-in-one gift and loyalty card that can be used at participating Tasti D-Lite locations.

Tasti trivia: Periodic contest held on Twitter that allows followers to interact and answer Tasti D-Lite–related trivia questions.

Tastimonial: Similar to a testimonial, Tastimonials are customer quotes that may appear on website pages for Tasti D-Lite locations.

TastiPad: iPad-based informational and interactive customer kiosks in use at participating Tasti D-Lite locations.

TastiRewards: The award-winning Tasti D-Lite loyalty program that allows members to earn rewards for their purchases and features integration with social networks Facebook, foursquare, and Twitter.

technological leapfrogging: As it relates to the implementation of new technologies, this kind of leapfrogging takes place when new and more advanced solutions are deployed soon after another was developed. In other words, a technology investment can quickly become outdated by the arrival of newer (and usually cheaper) solutions in the time it took to design and implement the first solution.

tweetup: An in-person "meet-up" or physical social gathering of Twitter users.

Twittersphere: The virtual space where the conversation between Twitter users takes place.

Urban Dictionary: A website that provides definitions for slang words and phrases. It is run by volunteer editors and rated by users of the site. See http://urbandictionary.com.

wall of happiness: A large bulletin board at the Tasti D-Lite home office containing creative and happy tweets from Tasti D-Lite customers.

INDEX

ABOUT THE AUTHORS

JIM AMOS
Chairman and CEO
of Tasti D-Lite LLC

Chairman and CEO, James Amos, Jr., acquired Tasti D-Lite in 2007 with New York-based private equity firm Snow Phipps Group. Jim has assembled a world-class franchising team with the goal of opening 500 centers globally. In 2011, Planet Smoothie was acquired to be integrated into the Planet Tasti platform.

Before Tasti D-Lite, Jim was the CEO of Mailboxes, Etc., the world's largest nonfood franchise, which is now the UPS Store. He grew MBE from 2,500 to 4,000 locations in 80 countries, making it the world's largest and fastest-growing franchisor of retail business, communication, and postal service centers. Jim was chairman of the IFA in 2001 and gained experience in the frozen dessert category through building a 2,500-store network for "I Can't Believe It's Yogurt!"

A former Marine Corps captain and veteran of two combat tours in Vietnam, Jim received 12 decorations, including the Purple Heart and Vietnamese Cross of Gallantry. A graduate of the University of Missouri, he is the author of several books including the bestsellers *The Memorial*, *Focus or Failure: America at the Crossroads*, and *The Complete Idiot's Guide to Franchising*.

Jim has served on or is serving on the board of directors of the National Veteran's Administration, the Marine Military Academy, the Marine Corps Heritage Foundation, Meineke Car Care Centers, Oreck Corporation, Zig Ziglar Corporation, WSI of Canada, the University of Missouri, the HealthStore Foundation, and Ken Blanchard's Faith Walk Leadership Foundation. He is currently chairman of Procter & Gamble's franchising arm, Agile Pursuits Franchising, Inc.

In 2011, Jim's leadership in the franchising industry was recognized with his induction into the International Franchise Association Hall of Fame.

BJ EMERSON
Vice President,
Technology,
Tasti D-Lite LLC

BJ's curious blend of creative and technical abilities can be seen through the innovative solutions and campaigns he manages. His consistent track record of innovation and leadership includes overseeing the rapid expansion of technologies for entire franchise networks. In 2005, BJ led the deployment of a $2 million corporate and franchise enterprise technology platform which won a Microsoft Pinnacle Award for excellence in 2006.

As an early social technology navigator, BJ's unique perspective comes in part through introducing the Tasti D-Lite brand into online communities and ultimately integrating those with the award-winning TastiRewards loyalty platform.

His early and revolutionary use of mobile coupons on Twitter earned Tasti D-Lite a spot in Twitter's Business 101 Case Studies which led to invitations for Tasti D-Lite to be launch partners with business products for companies such as foursquare and Google.

BJ's projects have been featured as case studies in several different books published in 2011. Also, he provided the foreword to *Location Based Marketing for Dummies*.

A veteran of the first gulf war, BJ has the U.S. Navy to thank for his solid foundation in technology, which was followed by several years of successful small-business ownership.

BJ currently sits on the board of SNAP Services, LLC, which is the first social network appreciation platform to enable businesses to bring together point-of-sale transactions and digital word-of-mouth customer rewards.

Regularly quoted in major publications and other media, BJ speaks throughout the United States as well as internationally on a regular basis on the topics of social media, technology, and customer loyalty.